MW01620420

BASIC READING SERIES / Level E

Kittens and Children

by Donald Rasmussen and Lynn Goldberg

SCIENCE RESEARCH ASSOCIATES, INC.
Chicago, Palo Alto, Toronto
Henley-on-Thames, Sydney, Paris, Stuttgart
A Subsidiary of IBM

Printed in the United States of America.

ISBN: 0-574-45950-2

Illustrator:

Joseph Rogers

Contributors:

Penny Baker
Ann Bishop
Beatrice Brittain Braden
William Braden
John Dennis
Bryce Engle
Jeane Engle
Justin M. Fishbein
Hal Higdon
Jeanne Hopp
Kay W. Levin
Selma Levinger
Annie Moldafsky
George R. Paterson
Barbara Polikoff
Enid Levinger Powell
Enid Warner Romanek
John Savage

Contents

Section 9

__ ed

bat	end	lift	nod	hunt
batted	ended	lifted	nodded	hunted

__ ed

tag	spell	fill	rob	club
tagged	spelled	filled	robbed	clubbed

__ ed

rap	peck	mix	chop	brush
rapped	pecked	mixed	chopped	brushed

__ es

catch	dress	fix	box	buzz
catches	dresses	fixes	boxes	buzzes

__ er

bat	lend	fix	box	buzz
batter	lender	fixer	boxer	buzzer
■	■	■	■	■
sad	fresh	sick	fond	gruff
sadder	fresher	sicker	fonder	gruffer
■	■	■	■	■
matter	better	bitter	copper	butter
scatter	letter	litter	proper	gutter
shatter	■	■	chopper	clutter
	never	liver		
■			■	shutter
banner	ever	river	bother	
				stutter
			■	
manner		shiver		■
			robber	
■		■		summer
gather		silver		
				■
rather				supper
■				■
ladder				rubber
■				
after				

__ est, __ ness

sad	fresh	sick	fond	gruff
■	■	■	■	■
sadder	fresher	sicker	fonder	gruffer
saddest	freshest	sickest	fondest	gruffest
■	■	■	■	■
sadness	freshness	sickness	fondness	gruffness

__ en

fat	red	stiff	rot	sunk
fatten	redden	stiffen	rotten	sunken
■	■	■		■
happen	seven	bitten	gotten	sudden
■		kitten	■	
Allen		mitten	oxen	
		■		
		linen		
		■		
		chicken		
		■		
		children		
		■		
		kitchen		

That's My Grandmother!

My grandmother said,
"You're so much thinner!
I know what's the matter.
I'll fix you a dinner."

"No," I said, "Grandmother,
Forget the matter."
"Yes," said my grandmother,
"You SHOULD be fatter."

She stuffed a plump chicken
With figs from her shelf,
And crackers and plums.
Then I stuffed myself.

My grandmother fed me
The best chicken dinner.
Then Grandmother said to me,
"You should be thinner."

The Cat That Quacked

A fisherman had a cat and it had seven kittens. Six of the kittens were just what you'd think they'd be. They acted just as other kittens do.

But the seventh kitten didn't. It was a quacking kitten.

"QUACK," said the seventh kitten. "QUACK. QUACK. QUACK."

The kitten's mother couldn't understand this. And the fisherman couldn't understand it.

Whenever the fisherman couldn't understand something, it bothered him.

"You shouldn't quack," said the fisherman.

"QUACK," said the kitten.

"Ducks quack," said the fisherman. "Kittens don't."

"QUACK," said the kitten.

"No, no, NO!" said the fisherman. "It's not proper. It just isn't done."

"QUACK," said the kitten.

"Stop that quacking," said the fisherman, "or I'll get rid of you. I'll drop you in the river."

The kitten scratched itself and licked its whiskers.

"QUACK," it said.

So the fisherman picked up the kitten and flung it into the river.

"There!" said the fisherman.

And he rushed off. He was glad to be rid of the quacking kitten.

Just after the fisherman left, a ragman passed by. The ragman got a stick and helped the kitten from the river.

The kitten dripped and shivered. Then it blinked at the ragman and said:

"QUACK."

"Well, well," said the ragman. "A quacking kitten." The ragman wasn't bothered by things he didn't understand.

He picked up the wet kitten.

"Do you want some dinner?" he asked. "Come with me if you wish."

"QUACK," said the kitten. So the ragman went off with the kitten. He fed it scraps from his supper and milk from a pitcher. And after that, the kitten slept under a bench in the ragman's kitchen.

Spring, summer, and winter passed.

The kitten got bigger and bigger, till it was a cat. But it still quacked.

"Anyone can have a cat," said the ragman. "But I have something better—a cat that quacks!"

The ragman had a sister, and his sister had a plan. "You should sell this cat," she said. "There's not another quacking cat in the land. You could sell it and get rich."

"No," said the ragman. "I would never sell my cat. Never!"

But he stopped to think.

"I know what I'll do," he said. "I'll sell a pass to anyone who wants to pet my cat."

So the ragman got a box with a slot in the top. And he printed some passes. The passes said in big letters:

PET THE QUACKING CAT

HERE

JUST ONE IN THE LAND

And what do you think happened? Mothers and fathers and children rushed to the ragman's kitchen. They dropped silver into the box and got passes. And they went in to pet the quacking cat.

By the end of summer the ragman and his sister were rich.

And at last, who came by to pet the cat? The fisherman himself!

"Your quacking cat has helped you get rich," he said to the ragman. "And let me tell you something odd. I had a quacking kitten myself. If I'd kept it, I'd be as rich as you are!"

"You should have kept it," said the ragman.

"Yes," said the fisherman, "but I can't understand it. Why will anyone spend cash to pet a quacking cat? There are quacking ducks. And no one ever spent anything to pet a quacking duck."

"That's so," said the ragman. "But there are lots of quacking ducks, and there is just one quacking cat. A quacking duck isn't anything. But a quacking cat—that IS something."

"It is," said the fisherman. "But I don't know why."

"I don't understand it myself," said the ragman.

Can you understand it?

Summer Swimmer

I don't shudder, quiver, shiver
As I spring into the river.
I'm a splashing summer swimmer
   Having fun.

Silver fishes blink and scatter.
They must chatter, "What's the matter?"
They don't know I'm just a swimmer
   In the sun.

I am quicker than the flicker
Of a silver fish's fin.
When it's summer at the river
   I go summer-swimming in.

The King Who Never Slept

There was, in the past, a king who never slept.

He wanted to. But he couldn't.

Whenever he began to rest, something would happen.

A duck would quack. Or the plaster would crack.

A fly would buzz.

Or a pin would drop.

Someone would shiver. Or a dog would scratch itself. Or a kitten would lick its whiskers.

Someone would go thump, bump, or plump. Or something would go plink, plank, or plop.

The king would get mad and jump up from his bed.

"Be still!" he would cry. "I can't rest with this quacking and cracking! I can't stand this scratching and licking!

"I won't put up with this thumping, bumping, and plumping—this plinking, planking, and plopping!"

The king sent for his helpers. "Go into the land," he said. "Tell the mothers, fathers, and children to be still. Tell the chickens and kittens and ducks and so on just to stop it! I'm the king, and I won't be bothered in this manner."

It wasn't fun to be still. But the king was king, and you had to do what the king said.

So no one hammered. No one thumped, bumped, or plumped. No one plinked, planked, or plopped.

A hush fell on the land. There was not so much as a whisper.

"That's better," said the king.

And he crept back into his bed. But just as he began to rest, a clap of thunder crashed in the sky.

The king jumped up.

"What was that?" he yelled.

"That?" said someone. "Why, that was thunder."

"Thunder?" said the king. "Well, don't just stand there! Shut it off!"

But the king's helpers couldn't shut off the thunder.

The king was so mad that his helpers shivered.

"Don't just stand there shivering!" he said. "Go into the land and get me someone who can shut off that thunder. The one who shuts it off shall have a chest of silver."

The king's helpers went into the land as the king said they must. They hunted and hunted for someone to stop the thunder. But no one could do as the king had asked.

"Go back," said the king. "Tell them that anyone who shuts off the thunder shall have TWO chests of silver."

But no one could do it.

"Offer them SEVEN chests of silver," said the king.

But still no one could do it—not for two chests of silver or for seven.

The king couldn't understand why his helpers were so helpless. "I'll have to do it myself," he said.

He sent a helper to bring him a ladder.

"And be prompt," he added.

The helper was back in a wink with a stepladder.

"No, no," said the king. "I want a big ladder. I want the biggest ladder there is."

So the helpers got one ladder and added it to another. They did that till they had the biggest ladder there ever was.

"That's better," said the king.

He tested the ladder and stepped up on it.

"I'll be back," he said. "I'll be back when I've shut off the thunder."

And he went up the ladder—up one rung after another—into the sky.

He went up. But he has not yet come back.

It could be that he will never come back.

No one can tell.

But after the king left, a duck began to quack. A dog scratched itself. A kitten licked its whiskers.

Children began to skip and hop. Some yelled. Some sang. They chopped and scratched and splashed. They clumped and stamped. They hammered and plastered.

In fact, they still do.

Kittens and Children

What do kittens do?
  They stretch and scratch and splash.
Just as children do,
  They spring and twist and dash.

Kittens scrap with one another
  Just as children do.
And when the thunder thunders,
  Kittens scat, they do.

But kittens don't have mittens
  Or rubbers when it's wet.
And children don't have whiskers.
  (Or they don't have them yet!)

The Slickest, Quickest Pet

Jasper was my grasshopper,
  Last summer's swiftest pet,
The slickest, quickest grasshopper
  That I had ever met.

He'd gather up his legs to stretch,
  As if to test his wings,
And jump a sudden, flying jump,
  As if his legs had springs.

When Jasper sat and scratched himself,
I'd catch him in my hands
And put him in a grass-filled box
Held shut by rubber bands.

I've never had a better pet.
I am so glad I met him—
Last summer's slickest, quickest pet,
I never will forget him.

— y				
dad	pep	Bill	rock	pup
daddy	peppy	Billy	rocky	puppy

— ly				
sad	fresh	swift	hot	glum
sadly	freshly	swiftly	hotly	glumly

— ily				
happy			sloppy	lucky
▪			▪	▪
happily			sloppily	luckily

— ies, — ied				
pansy	empty	lily	copy	study
pansies	empties	lilies	copies	studies
	▪		▪	▪
	emptied		copied	studied

__le

candle
handle
■
fiddle
middle
riddle
■
pickle
tickle

twinkle
sprinkle
■
mumble
tumble
grumble

apple
■
saddle
■
little
■
bottle
■
gobble
■
uncle

__el

gravel
travel
■
camel
■
flannel
■
level
■
nickel
■
tunnel

__al

medal
pedal
■
metal
petal
■
signal

__ful

thank	rest	fist	box	cup
thankful	restful	fistful	boxful	cupful

__on

wagon
dragon
■
cannon
■
gallon
■
melon

__in

napkin
■
pumpkin
■
robin

__ain

captain

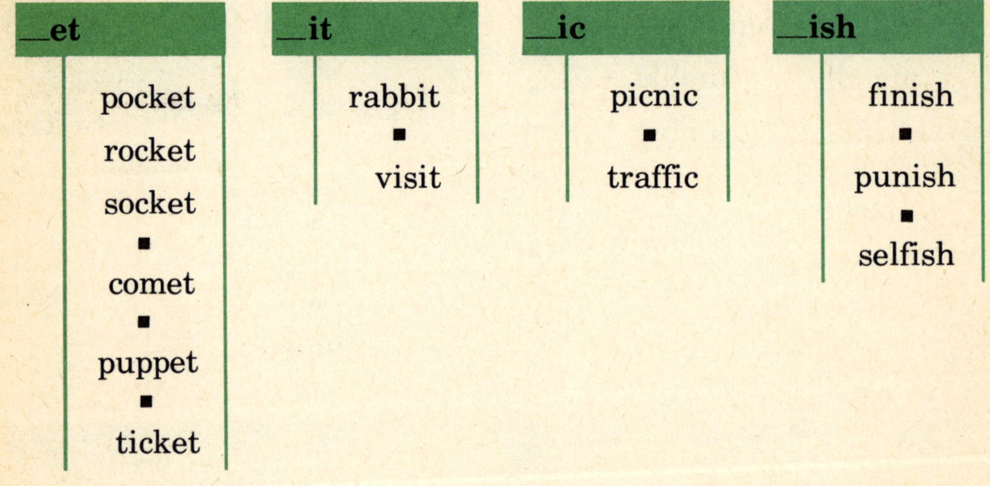

__et	__it	__ic	__ish
pocket rocket socket ■ comet ■ puppet ■ ticket	rabbit ■ visit	picnic ■ traffic	finish ■ punish ■ selfish

Picnic

Summer sun.
  Jolly fun.
Picnic basket.
  Go get one.

Chicken! Yum!
  Pickles! Yum!
Want a radish?
  Here, have some.

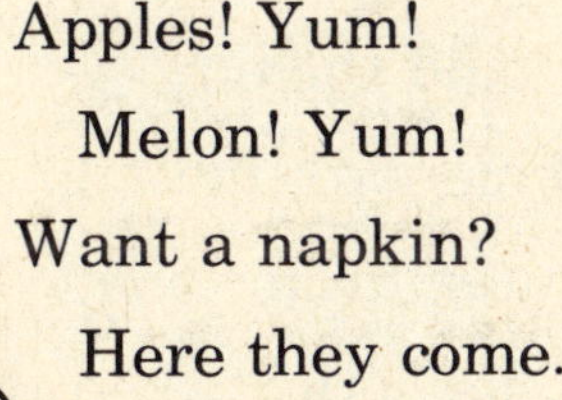

Apples! Yum!
  Melon! Yum!
Want a napkin?
  Here they come.

Many ants.
  Rip in pants.
Just a sprinkle
  Helps the plants.

Summer sun.
  Jolly fun.
We are happy.
  Picnic's done.

The Elf

On a blanket on the grass
  Sat a funny little elf.
It gobbled and it nibbled
  At a picnic by itself.

A jolly little rabbit
  Hopped up to the little elf,
Saying, "Can I picnic with you?
  Why nibble by yourself?"

"Yes," said the elf,
  "Nibble with me—do!
A picnic's fun for one,
  But it's better when there's two."

Blossom the Skunk

Blossom was a little skunk. She was glad that winter had ended and that it was spring. She was so glad that she ran up the hill, hunting for someone to have fun with.

A dog was on the hill, sitting by the pond. Blossom ran up to him and said, "Why don't we run and have some fun?" But the dog just ran on up the hill as fast as he could.

Then Blossom spotted a rabbit nibbling radishes. She went up to the rabbit, but he ran off.

Next Blossom ran up to some cattle that were munching the grass. But when they spotted Blossom, they scattered.

"What can be the matter?" Blossom said. "Why won't they have anything to do with me?"

After that Blossom met a cat, an elk, a hen, and a rat. But they dashed off when Blossom ran up.

Blossom went back to her den, sobbing.

"What's the matter, Blossom?" asked her mother. "Why are you so sad?"

"Nobody will have anything to do with me," said Blossom. "They run whenever I come by. I just want to be with them and have fun. I don't understand."

Blossom's mother sat thinking, and then she said:

"It could be that they don't understand skunks, Blossom. The elk kicks when it gets mad, and the cat scratches. Well, we don't do such things. We DO smell bad if we're mad or if we think somebody is going to kill us. But that doesn't happen much. If they could understand this, they would be your pals."

When Blossom went to bed she felt much better. She got up with the sun and rushed off to tell somebody what her mother had said. Presently she met Janet the cat.

"Janet," Blossom said, "I have something to tell you."

Janet sniffed, backed off, and said, "What could you tell me that I don't know?"

"I bet you don't know that skunks don't smell bad. That is, they just smell bad when they're mad or think somebody is after them."

"No, I didn't know that," said Janet. She sniffed. "I don't smell a thing."

"What did I tell you!" said Blossom. "You do something that isn't very proper when you get mad. You scratch. I don't scratch when I'm mad; I just smell bad. But we can still have fun and be pals."

"So we can!" said Janet. "I'm so sorry, Blossom. And I'm going to go with you to tell the others."

So Blossom and Janet went to the pond. The elk, the hen, the rat, the dog, and the rabbit were there, drinking.

"Quick, here comes you know who," yelped the dog.

"I smell a skunk," said the rabbit as he began to hop off.

Janet jumped up on a rock and said:

"No you don't, Mr. Rabbit. You just think you do. Blossom just smells bad when she's mad. What do the rest of you do when you get mad? The elk kicks and the hen pecks. And we know that the rat and the dog bit the rabbit when they got mad at him.

"We should be sorry for running from Blossom. I, for one, am going to be her pal."

"I'm sorry, Blossom," said the rabbit.

"So am I," said the dog. "We just didn't understand."

The others nodded. Blossom went with them for a romp on the grass. They had a lot of fun—and nobody got mad.

Jam and Jelly

Blackberry,
Cranberry,
Appleberry Sam.

He is
Fond of
Crackers and jam.

Tickleberry,
Pickleberry,
Nickelberry Nelly.

She is
Fond of
Milk and jelly.

Sam has his jam,
Nelly has her jelly,
But I want candy
To fill MY belly!

An Itch in the Middle

Said a camel to a doctor,
  "This tickle bothers me.
It's at the middle of my hump,
  And itches bitterly."

The doctor said, "Then scratch it."
  The camel said, "I try,
But my legs will not go back there."
  And he began to cry.

"I'm sorry," said the doctor.
  "I'll do what I can do.
I know it isn't funny
  When something itches you."

So the doc began to think,
  And she sang a little riddle:
"Hump and humperdink,
  The itch is in the middle."

The doctor said, "I think
  I know a little fly
Who's visiting a puppy
  And will be buzzing by."

"We'll ask the fly," the doctor said,
  "To sit on top of you
And scratch your little middle-itch
  Just when you tell it to."

"Well, thank you," said the camel.
  "Well, thank you," said the fly.
They are a happy twosome
  As they go scratching by.

__ **ee** __				
bee	feed	seen	deep	beet
see	need	green	keep	feet
wee	seed	queen	peep	meet
free	weed	screen	creep	sweet
tree	■	fifteen	sleep	street
three	feel	■	sweep	■
	heel	peek		seem
	wheel	seek		■
		week		needle
		cheek		■
				speech

— **ea** —				
pea	beat	team	meal	leaf
sea	heat	cream	real	■
tea	meat	dream	seal	leap
flea	neat	gleam	steal	■
■	seat	steam	■	weak
each	treat	scream	bean	■
beach	wheat	stream	lean	eager
peach	eat	■	mean	■
reach	■	beast	clean	eagle
teach	bead	feast		■
	lead	least		reason
	read	east		season
				■
				beaver

My Puppy

If I just had a penny,
  I can tell you what I'd get:
An eager little puppy
  That would want to be my pet.

He'd sleep on my green blanket,
  Where he'd cuddle by my feet.
And I would feed him anything
  He wanted, for a treat.

We'd run and romp and scramble,
  And if he scratched my hand,
He really would be sorry,
  And I would understand.

I'd keep my funny puppy,
  And he would never know
That I got him for a penny.
  I'd never let him go.

DOC
WHEELER

The Missing Sack

Cast:

Jean Reed

Doc Wheeler

Mrs. Dean

Jill Lee

Sam Lee

Jimmy Easter

Jean Reed (yelling into tent): Here's a Mrs. Dean to see you, Doc.

Doc Wheeler: Step into the tent, Mrs. Dean. *(Mrs. Dean comes in.)* It's a real treat to meet you. What can I do to help you?

Mrs. Dean: It isn't me that needs help, Doc. It's my little Betty. She wants to be a jumper on the track team.

Doc Wheeler: So let her be on the team. Why do you need me?

Mrs. Dean: There's just one thing—she can't jump well.

Doc Wheeler: So that's it. Mrs. Dean, I have what she needs. You just go back to Jean and get her to sell you a bottle of my Flea Cream.

Mrs. Dean: Flea Cream! My Betty doesn't have fleas! She just wants to jump better!

Doc Wheeler: Mrs. Dean, have you ever seen a flea jump? You just rub a little Doc Wheeler's Flea Cream on that Betty of yours, and she'll be jumping better in less than a week! She'll jump as well as a flea—or better. Fifteen, sixteen, seventeen feet!

Mrs. Dean (going): O thank you, Doc. And thank you from Betty and the track team.

Jean Reed (sending Jill and Sam Lee into the tent): Here are the Lees, Doc.

Jill Lee: It's my brother Sam who needs you, Doc. He just doesn't seem to have any pep. He doesn't feel eager to do anything. Not a thing seems to matter to him.

Doc Wheeler: Is that the problem, Sam? Want me to fix that up, do you?

Sam Lee: Not really. It doesn't matter much.

Doc Wheeler: Yep, he's got it bad. But I have just what he needs. Jill, get Jean to sell you a bag of Doc Wheeler's Beaver Feed. Feed him some with each meal, and he'll be eager, eager, EAGER! A real eager beaver! What do you think of THAT, Sam?

Sam Lee: Not much. Does it really matter?

Doc Wheeler (yelling to Jean): Jean, sell them some beaver feed and get rid of them. Who's next? *(Jill and Sam Lee go.)*

Jean Reed (sending Jimmy Easter into the tent): Jimmy Easter to see you, Doc.

Doc Wheeler: Don't be shy, Jimmy. Speak freely. Tell me what you need.

Jimmy Easter: It isn't what I NEED – it's what I've GOT. I've got an uncle who needs your help.

Doc Wheeler: Why does he need my help?

Jimmy Easter: Last week he sneaked into your tent and helped himself to a sack of something. After he'd eaten the stuff in the sack, he began to act funny. He's not himself.

Doc Wheeler (yelling to Jean): Jean—quick! See if anything's missing. Jimmy, what was in that sack?

Jimmy Easter: I don't know. The tag said "Doc Wheeler's . . ." something. I think it ended with "Feed."

Doc Wheeler: I see. And he didn't get any sweeter after he'd eaten it?

Jimmy Easter: No—a lot LESS sweet.

Doc Wheeler: Then it wasn't Bee Feed. Did you feel any heat when he said things? I mean, was there a hot wind from his lips?

Jimmy Easter: No.

Doc Wheeler: Then it wasn't Dragon Feed. Does he swim any better than he did?

Jimmy Easter: No.

Doc Wheeler: Then it wasn't Frogman Feed. Let's see . . . Does he get going on speeches?

Jimmy Easter: Yes! That's it!

Doc Wheeler: The speeches—do they have anything to do with the need to study? Does he tell you that you should spell better? Does he try to get you to read faster? And when you read something badly, does he tell you what the letters are? Does he ask you to have another try at it?

Jimmy Easter: Yes! Yes! That's him! Why does he act so odd?

Jean Reed (coming into the tent): Doc! Doc! A sack IS missing, and I know what was in it!

Doc Wheeler: So do I!

Jean Reed and Doc Wheeler: TEACHER FEED!

THE END

Peanuts the Pup

Jill and Dick and Ben were pals. They had a raft.

"Let's go on a trip," said Jill. "We can go up the stream on the raft."

"O.K.," said Ben. "I'll pack a lunch, and you two get the raft off the beach and into the stream."

Just then Dick's little dog, Peanuts, ran up to them. Peanuts was yelping eagerly.

"Do you have to bring Peanuts?" asked Jill. "He keeps yelping for no reason. He's such a bother."

"But he's my pet," said Dick. "Wherever I go, Peanuts can go."

"Well, O.K.," said Jill. "Come on, Peanuts."

Dick and Jill tugged and tugged till they got the raft into the stream.

"Here's Ben with the lunch," said Dick. "Off we go!"

They leaped onto the raft. Peanuts jumped on last. Jill and Dick didn't have paddles. But they had big sticks that reached the bottom of the stream.

They were having lots of fun. Peanuts sat in the middle of the raft and yelped and yapped.

Suddenly the raft began to drift into the deep middle of the stream. Then the sticks didn't reach the bottom!

Jill and Dick and Ben screamed for help.

Peanuts leaped into the stream and swam to the beach. Then he ran as fast as he could. He ran and ran till he met Mr. Wheeler.

Peanuts yelped and yapped at him. But Mr. Wheeler just said, "That dog never stops yelping." And he went on.

So Peanuts ran on till he met Mr. Green. He yelped at him. He leaped up on him and tugged at his pants cuff. Then he began to run back to the beach.

But Mr. Green just yelled at Peanuts. "You bad dog! You've got my pants muddy!"

It seemed to Peanuts that nobody could understand. He wished he could speak.

He ran on and on. Suddenly he spotted Mrs. Bean. Mrs. Bean didn't know that Peanuts yelped a lot for no reason.

Peanuts leaped up and put his wet feet on Mrs. Bean's slacks. He yipped and yipped.

"This dog seems to be telling me something," Mrs. Bean said. "What could it be? Does somebody need help?"

Peanuts ran to the beach, and Mrs. Bean ran after him. From the beach Mrs. Bean could see the raft. And she could see the three children clinging to it.

Mrs. Bean ran back for help. Then she and some others swam to the raft and picked up Dick and his pals.

Peanuts greeted them on the beach. And he was still yelping.

After that, nobody said anything when Peanuts yelped. They just grinned and petted him.

And whenever Dick went somewhere with his pals, one of them would yell, "Bring Peanuts!"

Lee's Bees

When Lee Wheeler finished the speech on her hobby, each member of her class said that her hobby was the best. She was a keeper of bees. "I didn't know we had a beekeeper in class," said Mr. Dean, the teacher. "When we wish to know something about bees, we know where to go!"

"Will you let us see your bees?" the class was eager to know.

"O, yes," said Lee. "My bees and I will be very happy to have you visit. If it is sunny, come this weekend. This is the best season to see the bees."

"But, Lee," said Jack Reed, "will your bees sting me if I come to see them? I don't want to get stung."

"It could happen. But it's very seldom that my bees get mad and sting anyone. Don't let it keep you from visiting us," said Lee.

"It won't," said Mr. Dean. "We will come on the bus after lunch."

The weekend was sunny, and Lee and her mother were happy to greet the bus with Mr. Dean and the class on it.

"I keep my bees in back of the shed where they are sheltered from the wind," said Lee. "Let's go there and see them."

When the class was in back of the shed, Lee added, "You can see that I have many, many bees. There is one queen bee that is bigger than the other bees."

Just as Lee said that, a bee buzzed by Mr. Dean's neck. Mr. Dean slapped at the bee and yelled, "I think the queen bee is after me." Mr. Dean missed the bee, but the swing got the bee mad. It happened so fast. The bee landed on Mr. Dean's back. Mr. Dean felt it and ran speedily to some trees. Lee had to act fast.

"Mr. Dean," Lee screamed, "don't go to the tree. That is a bee tree and there are some bees in it. Run to the stream."

Just as Mr. Dean reached the stream, he felt the sting of the bee. He leaped six feet and landed in the middle of the stream. He yelled, "She got me! She got me! The queen bee stung me!"

"No! No!" Lee yelled back. "The queen never stings, Mr. Dean. Grab my hand and step on dry land."

Dripping wet, Mr. Dean stepped from the stream and said, "I've never seen so many mean bees."

"The bees aren't as mean as they seem," said Lee. "You shouldn't have slapped at them."

"I know," said Mr. Dean. "Next time I see a little bee, I won't slap at it."

"Do you still feel the sting?" asked Lee.

"Not much," said Mr. Dean. "But I'm still wet."

"Something to eat will make you feel better," said Lee. "Let's all go in and have fresh peaches and cream."

Sal the Seal

Sal the Seal stretched on the beach,
Feeling weak and green.
She was the saddest, greenest seal
That I have ever seen.

"Sal," I asked, "why do you weep?
I know you have a reason.
You are the saddest, greenest seal
I've seen in any season."

"Well," said Sal, "I cannot sleep,
So beastly do I feel."
There never was a beast as sad
As this green, seasick seal.

"It's sad," said I, "to be a seal
That's seasick from the sea.
As any proper seal should know,
The sea's the spot to be.

"But Sal," I said, "I know it's so:
On seaweed you do feast.
You're not a sadly seasick seal,
But a seaweed-sick green beast.

"So think of this: You don't need weeds
To be a proper seal.
Just gobble up some little fish
When hunting for a meal."

Sal flipped her whiskers in a grin.
"Thanks," she said to me.
"No weed for me," and off she swam
Into the deep green sea.

— oo —				
moo	boom	boot	hoop	food
too	room	hoot	loop	■
zoo	bloom	root	scoop	roof
igloo	broom	toot	whoop	■
■	■	shoot		tooth
moon	cool			■
noon	tool			rooster
soon	spool			
spoon	stool			

__ ai __

fail	gain	brain	paid	daisy
hail	main	grain	■ maid	■ raisin
mail	pain	train	■ maiden	■ aim
nail	rain	chain	■ wait	
pail		plain	■ waiter	
rail		stain	■ waist	
sail				
tail				

__ ay __

bay	clay	crayon
day	play	
gay	gray	
hay	pray	
may	tray	
pay	stay	
say	spray	
way	stray	

My Tooth

It was a gray and rainy day—
  A Sunday afternoon—
When one top tooth of Ben's went CLICK!
  And dropped into his spoon.

"My, what a funny thing," he said.
  "My tooth is in a teaspoon!
And if another tooth should drop,
  This spoon would be a TEETHSPOON!"

The Mixed-up Zoo

Sal and I got off the train and there was the zoo. A man was in the ticket booth.

"Say, mister," Sal said, "what do we have to pay to see your zoo?"

"Not a thing," said the man. "I pay YOU."

"Really?" said Sal.

"Really," said the man. "Then I lead you in and tell you what each thing is."

"O.K. Come on, Ray," Sal said to me. "Maybe we'll see a green-tailed fuzzy-wuzzy in this zoo."

Well, wait till I tell you what we DID see! There was a pig cutting branches and twigs with his teeth. He was putting up a dam! And next to him was a beaver, sleeping in the mud in the noonday sun.

"What's the matter with that pig?" asked Sal. "He's as mixed-up as the beaver."

"That's not a pig," said the man. "It's a branch-cutting peaver. And next to it is a mud-sleeping big."

Next was a skunk with webbed feet. She was swimming on a pond, quacking at her little skunks.

"That's a skuck and her little skucks," said the man.

Just then we spotted an eagle playing in the pond. He was doing tricks for the children. He flapped his flippers and begged the children to clap. His trainer pitched fish to him from a pail, and he never failed to catch them.

"What a way for a seal—I mean an eagle—to act," said Sal.

"That's not a seal or an eagle," said the man. "It's a seagle."

"Get your cool peanuts on a bun!"

"Get your hot lemon punch!"

It was a man at a food stand. "Step up, children," he yelled. "Step up and have some treats."

So we did. And after we had some, he paid each of us a dollar. It WAS a mixed-up zoo!

We went on—past a red sheep running after a fox and an elk swinging by its tail from a branch. Sal blinked and said, "A shox after a feep and an elky in a tree. What could be next?"

Here's what was next: a camel sitting on a rail. It kept flapping its wings and saying:

"Cock-a-doodle-doo! Cock-a-doodle-doo!"

"A rooster?" I asked.

"A cooster," said Sal. "Let's go on to the next one."

But the mixed-up zoo was too much for me. "I'm getting mixed up myself," I said. "Let's go."

And we ran up the path to the train as fast as we could.

"Ray, Ray," someone was saying. It was my teacher. "Ray, what is three plus six?"

"Three plus six is thrix," I said.

"Not in this class, it isn't," my teacher said. "Ray, are you daydreaming?"

I had to stay after class to tell her.

Rusty, the Red Rooster

Rusty was a little red rooster who was happy that at last he could cock-a-doodle-doo. He was standing on a rail at noon one day. He put up his chin and went "Cock-a-doodle-doo. Cock-a-doodle-doo."

"No, Rusty, no, no," said his father. "Can't you understand? You cock-a-doodle-doo when the sun is coming up. Or you can do it if there is some other reason. You don't cock-a-doodle-doo whenever you want to."

Rusty ruffled his tail and said, "Why do you keep telling me to wait? It's so much fun to cock-a-doodle-doo! I just can't keep from saying it."

A hen said to Rusty's father, "You should punish that little rooster. What a pain in the neck! He bothers me when I'm laying eggs."

Soon Mr. Clay, who ran the chicken ranch, dumped some grain from a pail into the feeding trays. Rusty was so happy to have some food that he went "Cock-a-doodle-doo." He gobbled grain till it seemed he would pop. Then he went into the hay for an afternoon nap.

But his mother said, "Get up, Rusty. You must help the other chicks pick up twigs and clean up the pen."

"I'm too little for such big jobs," said Rusty. "I need to sleep, anyway. Let the others do it. Cock-a-doodle-doo."

"Who does he think he is?" said a big rooster. "He needs some training. When we were chicks we had to do what Mother or Father said."

Rusty's mother pecked Rusty on the neck, and he jumped up in pain. He began to clean up the pen.

Soon he forgot his job and began playing on a rail. He fell from the rail and landed with a splash in the middle of a drinking pan. He hadn't planned it that way. But it was fun. He got back up on the rail and jumped back into the pan. He forgot and cock-a-doodle-dooed.

His father ran up, grabbed Rusty by the neck, and said, "No, no. Don't play in the drinking pans. And don't cock-a-doodle-doo for no reason. You must be punished. Fly onto that rail and stay there till I say you can get off."

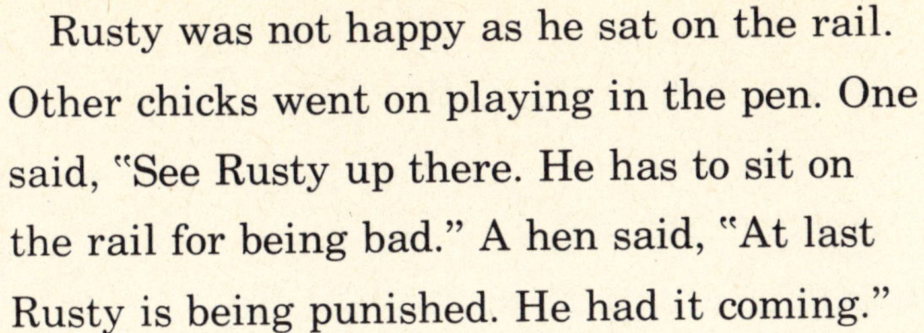

Rusty was not happy as he sat on the rail. Other chicks went on playing in the pen. One said, "See Rusty up there. He has to sit on the rail for being bad." A hen said, "At last Rusty is being punished. He had it coming."

Rusty just sat and sat on the rail. He was still sitting there when the moon was coming up. The other chickens were in the shed, sleeping. Rusty was thinking that his father had forgotten him, and he began to cry.

He was feeling sorry for himself when he happened to see the gray fox. The fox leaped into the pen. It jumped up, trying to catch Rusty's tail, but it couldn't reach him. Then the fox ran to the shed, where the other chickens were sleeping.

"We need help—fast!" Rusty said to himself. "Anybody knows a chicken is no match for a fox. I must do something.

"Cock-a-doodle-doo," screamed Rusty at the top of his lungs. The hens and roosters blinked. Seeing the fox, they began to scatter. The big roosters, too, began screaming "Cock-a-doodle-doo."

Soon Mr. Clay was running to the pen to see what was the matter. He ran after the fox with a broom, and it dashed off into the trees.

"If it wasn't for Rusty," said a big rooster, "that fox would have killed every one of us."

Rusty was so gay he just kept on saying "Cock-a-doodle-doo." And not one chicken in the pen could say that the little red rooster didn't have a reason.

Silver Kay Taylor

In May, it rained daily. The sky was gray and the sea was gray. No ships sailed into the Bay of Gulls. And the Inn of the Sea Maiden was empty too.

Nick, the Greek waiter at the inn, was upset that gloomy Sunday. He had fixed some food, but no one had come into the inn.

At two, Nick went to stand by the railing of the inn. There were no ships in the empty bay. Some gulls were crying sadly. On the beach, fishing nets swayed in the wind.

Nick leaned on his broom. The sea spray peppered his cheeks. He shivered.

"It's silly to be so gloomy," he said to himself. "It's just this grayness and rain that keeps a man thinking of foolish things."

Nick shrugged and stepped back into the empty room.

But the room wasn't empty! An odd, stooped man sat on a red stool.

His back was to Nick, but Nick could see that the man wasn't a sailor. His hat was big and black, and his boots were too gay. The sash at his waist was plainly silk.

"What can I do for you today?" Nick asked.

The man spun on his stool. A dagger gleamed at his waist.

Nick shivered.

"My sailors and I have strayed into your bay," the man said. "That fool at the wheel will pay for this," he hissed.

"Where is your ship?" Nick asked.

"In your bay," the man said. "We ran into shooting two days back. We ripped the sail and cracked the boom."

"Your ship is in the bay?" Nick asked. "But the bay is empty. No ships have sailed into the Bay of Gulls for days."

"O?" the man jumped up. "You do not see well, waiter?" He put his hand to his waist, then dropped it. "You're lucky," he said coolly. "Today is not my day to deal with playful waiters."

Nick was bothered by the man's manner. Why was this man so grim and moody?

The man dropped back onto his stool.

"Just get me some food, waiter," he said. "I'm a bit faint."

He put some silver on Nick's tray. "This should pay for it," he said.

Nick studied the silver on the tray. Silver such as this was never seen at the Inn of the Sea Maiden. Nick was never paid with such silver. He shrugged and scooped it into his pocket.

"Waiter, be quick!" the man snapped. "I must have food. Then you must get me a steed. I must go quickly, for they will soon be on my trail."

"A steed!" Nick said. "You must be kidding me!"

The man leaped to his feet. "Waiter, there is not room under this roof for you and me!" He reached for the dagger at his waist.

"Plainly this man is mad or a fool," Nick said to himself.

Someone's feet were stamping in the next room.

"Stay!" the man hissed. He pressed the tip of the dagger to Nick's chest. "Stay very still."

"Nick? Say, Nick, where are you? It's so gloomy in this room I can't see."

It was Spooner, the bay master.

Nick felt the tip of the gleaming dagger pressing his chest. He couldn't yell to Spooner. What could he do?

Suddenly Nick jumped back and stooped. There was a pail at his feet. He kicked it. The pail bumped the stools with a clang.

Nick felt the whish of a damp wind. He got to his feet as Spooner rushed into the room. The room was empty.

"Nick, are you okay?"

"Yes," said Nick. "But where did he go?"

"Go? Who?" asked Spooner. "There's no one here, and no one passed me. What are you saying, Nick? The gloomy days must be getting to you, too."

"But he was here," Nick said. "An odd, stooped man. He had a dagger at his waist. He said funny things, too."

"Dagger at his waist?" Spooner studied Nick. "You see men with daggers at the waist in paintings—not today."

Nick nodded. "But he was here."

Spooner went on, "Not that plenty of men with daggers haven't stayed in this inn," he said. "In days past, sea raiders would come here. The innkeeper helped them. They say Silver Kay Taylor himself sailed into this bay. His ship had a ripped sail and a cracked boom. He got food in this very room. Then he galloped off. The mayor's men were after him. But they didn't get him. That was the last that was ever seen of him."

"No," said Nick, feeling the silver in his pocket, "not the last."

The Sleepy Rooster

One Sunday in May
A rooster said,
"I think I'd rather
Stay in bed.

"Let another rooster
Cock-a-doodle-doo.
I think I would rather
Be a fool and moo.

"Or maybe I'll buzz,
Or bay at the moon.
Or maybe I'll just
Stay in bed till noon."

And so the rooster
Lay in the hay,
And said, "I'll have
A restful day."

"O, Rooster, Rooster,"
Said a snail,
"You must not wait,
You must not fail.

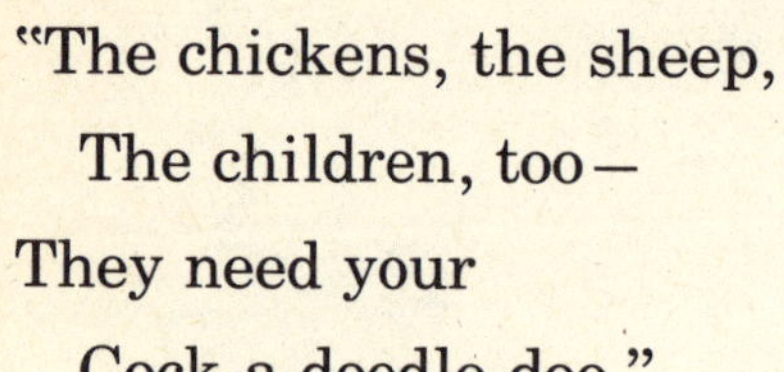

"The chickens, the sheep,
The children, too–
They need your
Cock-a-doodle-doo."

The rooster said,
"It's such a pain,
Cock-a-doodle-dooing
For my grain."

"But who needs a rooster,"
The little snail said,
"If he sleeps till noon
In a haystack bed?

"Who wants a rooster
Who'd rather play?
We'll get a better one,
Anyway."

The rooster screamed,
"You wait there, Snail!
I was just resting,
But I won't fail."

The rooster got up
And ran from the hay,
And cock-a-doodle-dooed
To signal day.

__oa__					
	boat	boast	coal	coach	soap
	coat	coast	goal	roach	■
	goat	roast	■	■	loaf
	float	toast	load	loan	■
	■		road	moan	roam
	oats		toad		

__ou__				
loud	found	pout	mouth	fountain
cloud	hound	shout	south	mountain
proud	pound	trout		
	round	out		
	sound			
	ground			

__ow__				
cow	down	power	howl	crowd
bow	gown	tower	growl	■
how	town	flower	owl	powder
now	brown	shower		■
sow	clown			towel
	crown			

Loudmouth, the Grasshopper

"I can outjump anybody in town," boasted the grasshopper. "In fact, I may be the best jumper in any town!"

He boasted so much that everyone began to speak of him as "Loudmouth, the grasshopper."

But that didn't bother Loudmouth. He was proud.

"Say what you want to. You just wish you had my powerful legs. Can anyone outjump me? Does anyone want to try?"

But nobody wanted to test the grasshopper.

One day the grasshopper hopped out of town. He hopped south, down a mountain road. He got to a stream. Mr. Toad was there with a towel on his back.

"How are you, Loudmouth?" asked Mr. Toad. "I'm out to swim and stretch my legs."

He put his towel on the ground and jumped into the stream. He began to swim and kick.

"Well, Mr. Toad, you're not a bad jumper yourself," said the grasshopper. "But I'm the best jumper in town."

"You boast too much, Loudmouth," the brown toad said as he floated in the stream.

"I'll bet I can jump from the bottom of this oak tree to that branch," the grasshopper said. "Must be at least ten feet. Why, I'll bet I can jump from the ground to the top of the fountain downtown."

Now the toad was getting sick of the grasshopper's boasting. And without thinking he said, "O.K., Loudmouth. You be here at noon, and we'll have a jumping match."

The grasshopper was as happy as he could be. But Mr. Toad wasn't happy as he hopped down the road to town.

"What's the frown for?" an owl shouted to Mr. Toad.

"I got sick of Loudmouth's boasting," said Mr. Toad, "so I boasted back. Now we have a jumping match at noon. And anybody knows a grasshopper can outjump a toad."

"Maybe I can coach you," the owl said. "After you leap, stretch out your legs and you'll sail a bit."

Mr. Toad said he'd try. He leaped and kept his legs stretched out. And he did jump better than ever.

"Keep trying," said the owl as she began to fly off. "And don't eat a thing. You'll jump better if you're not loaded down with food."

The owl went back to the stream where the grasshopper was.

"Well, Loudmouth," she said, "Mr. Toad tells me you two have a jumping match at noon."

"Yes," said Loudmouth, "but I can outjump a toad any day."

"I don't know," said the owl. "He's down the road eating. He's stuffing himself so his legs will be powerful."

"Is that so?" said Loudmouth.

"That's so," said the owl. "I'll be back at noon to see who wins."

Loudmouth gobbled up some oats, some grass, and two sunflowers. Then he felt so sleepy that he lay down to rest.

At noon the owl, the goat, the cow, and the rest of the crowd gathered for the jumping match. They found the grasshopper sleeping by the oak tree. The goat shouted, "Get up, Loudmouth. Let's see you jump." The grasshopper blinked in the sun, got up, and bowed to the crowd.

The two got set on the ground. The owl sat on the branch of the oak tree and began to count. She shouted, "One, two, three . . . go!"

Mr. Toad leaped – stretching out his legs as the owl had said he should.

The grasshopper wound up his legs – and jumped. He counted on winning – just as he had said he would.

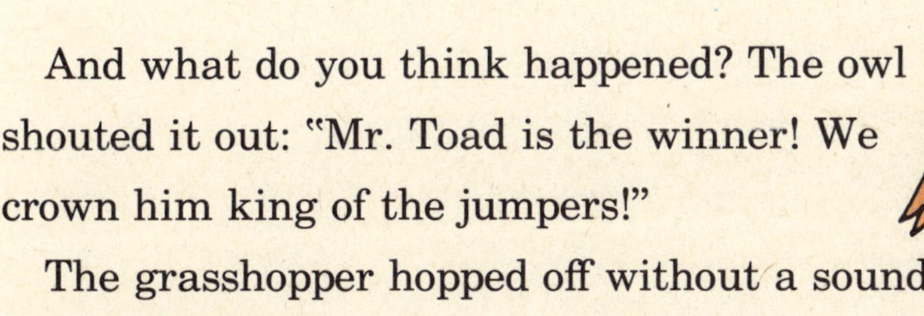

And what do you think happened? The owl shouted it out: "Mr. Toad is the winner! We crown him king of the jumpers!"

The grasshopper hopped off without a sound. The grasshopper is still in town. But he doesn't boast now. And nobody speaks of him as Loudmouth.

But nobody asks him for a jumping match. For anybody knows a grasshopper is the best jumper – if he isn't loaded down with food.

The Silly Sunflower

One day in a little
  Mountain town,
A sunflower gained
  The flowers' crown.

"I'm queen of the flowers,"
  She boasted out loud.
"I'm queen," she shouted,
  "And am I proud!"

"O no," a toad growled
  From on the ground.
"How can I sleep
  With that loud sound?"

"O my," said an owl,
  Floating down.
"How could they crown
  That loud, silly clown?"

A big brown cow
   Was coming down
To drink at the fountain
   In the town.

The sunflower bowed
   And said, "Now, Cow,
I'm queen of the flowers.
   I'm queen – and how!"

The brown cow smoothed
   Her coat and bowed,
And said, "Then I
   Am really proud
To eat a flower
   That's queen of the crowd."
And that's what she got
   For being so loud.

Why I'm Here

Chapter 1

It's the end of summer, and I've sat at this bus stop from the tenth of May till now. I may go on sitting here till NEXT May if I don't have some luck soon.

I was waiting for a bus back in May, with seven nickels in my pocket. (They were to pay for the bus.) Next to me was a man with this big, big basket on his back. So I asked him what he had in the basket. And he said:

"Steamboat sails!
 Jellied snails!
  Leaky oatmeal pails!
Fifty-pound hammers
 and twenty-inch nails!"

And he wanted to sell me some of each.

I said I didn't want any of the things he'd listed, and I asked if he had anything better. He said he had:

"Toadstool legs!
  Beavers' trousers!
    Rain-soaked rugs!
  And sixty-three bottles
  of zippy little bugs!"

And he said he'd sell them cheap.

I said they weren't just what I needed. So he went on. He said his basket held:

"Daisy chains!
  Trash from trains!
    Clumsy mountain goats!
  Seventeen screech owls
  with dry, scratchy throats!"

"No," I said, "I don't think I can do much with any of that. But thanks for telling me."

A bus stopped, and I was going to get on it. But the man wasn't finished with his list. He went on, getting louder and louder:

"Cloudy dreams!
Shy moonbeams!
Teaspoonsful of goos!
And fifty-six hundred
Yankee-doodle-doos!"

Well, the bus left without me, and I could tell that the man's stuff was getting better as he went on.

"How much for a moonbeam?" I asked.

"The best ones sell for a dollar fifty," he said. "Little dim ones are just a dollar."

But I didn't have a dollar—just my seven nickels for the bus. So I asked him how much Yankee-doodle-doos were. (I forgot to ask him WHAT they were.)

"Three for a dollar," he said. "They come in threes, and I can't split them up. So you have to get at least three." So that was out.

I just said, "Well, it's a swell basket of stuff, but I don't have ——"

"A swell BASKET—yes!" he said. "You want the basket? It's yours for just seven nickels."

Well! As I said, I DID have seven nickels. And it was such a swell basket, I wanted it for my mom. She had said she needed a basket.

So, forgetting the bus, I said "O.K." And I handed him my seven nickels.

Chapter 2

The man put down the basket and was going to trot off.

"Wait," I shouted. "You left everything in it!"

"Well, I HAVE to, don't I?" he shouted back. "How can I lug that stuff without any basket to keep it in? If I let you have the basket, I'll just have to let you have what's in it too."

"But I haven't paid you for what's in it," I said.

"Yes, and that's too bad," he said. "It's a bad deal for me. But a deal is a deal."

"But what am I going to do with this nutty stuff ?" I asked.

"That's what I kept asking myself, too," he said. "I kept trying to sell it, but nobody wanted any of it. Now you've ended my problem. I'm rid of it, and I have seven nickels. I think I'll get on the bus."

Another bus had stopped, and he got on it. It left, and that was that.

So that's why I'm sitting at this bus stop with this big basket. What can I do? There's so much stuff in it, I can't get it up on my back and go off with it.

And I can't dump the stuff out on the street and just keep the empty basket. That would be littering the streets. I could be put in jail if I did that.

And I can't just go off and let it stay here. I mean, I paid seven nickels for it, so how can I just go off and forget it? If I did that, I wouldn't have ANYTHING!

And I have to get my seven nickels back, so I can get on a bus!

So that's why I've waited at this bus stop for seventeen weeks, shouting:

"Steamboat sails!
Jellied snails!
Leaky oatmeal pails!
Fifty-pound hammers
and twenty-inch nails!"

But nobody wants any. Do you, mister? Do you want some toadstool legs? beavers' trousers? rain-soaked rugs? Want to try a bottle of zippy little bugs?

The Boastful Goat

Next to a little town there was a very big mountain. A road wound round and round the mountain. But the mountain was so big, and the road was so steep, that no one in the town could go up it.

Now in the town next to the mountain, there was a goat. He was the loudest, proudest goat anywhere. He couldn't say a thing without boasting. The goat said he could do anything better than anybody.

If someone counted to ten, he said he could count to twenty. If someone plowed a bit of ground, he said he could plow a bigger bit—better. If someone picked a pink flower, he said he could pick a pinker one.

Counting, plowing, picking—the boastful goat boasted he could do each one best. He would boast, then grin, then bow. From sunup to sundown, that's how it went. Everyone was sick of his boasting.

Now, one day, the boastful goat happened to see a toad. The toad jumped up on a toadstool.

"O," said the boastful goat, "how silly you are. Being on top of a toadstool doesn't count for much. A toadstool is so little."

"Well," said the toad, "I'm little. It's a pretty big jump for someone as little as I am. You're big. If I were as big as you, I could jump to that rock way up there. Can you do better than that?" asked the toad.

So the goat said, "I can do much better than that. I can outdo you, toad. Why, I can outdo anyone. I can jump to that rock way up there. And then I can jump up to the next rock. And then to the NEXT one. Why, I can jump till I'm up where no one in this town can go!"

Then the goat grinned proudly and bowed.

The toad jumped down from the toadstool.

"Can you jump to the top of the mountain?" asked the toad.

"Yes," said the goat, "I can jump to the top of the mountain. I can jump to where the clouds are."

"Wow!" said the toad. "May I see you do it?"

Now the goat didn't know what to say. No one had ever asked him to do what he said he could do. No one had ever asked him to count to twenty or to plow a bit of ground. No one had ever asked him to pick a pink flower.

"Well . . ." said the goat.

"Well?" said the toad.

The boastful goat didn't want the toad to think he was a coward. So what could he say?

"Well," said the goat, "I'll do it. Yes, I'll do it. And you can see me do it." And he bowed. But he didn't grin. He frowned.

"I can do anything," the goat growled.

"I can do anything better than anyone."

"WOW!" said the toad.

"I can do it," said the goat. And so he began.

He jumped to the big rock, way up there. It wasn't really a very big jump. But it seemed big to the toad, who was so little.

On the next jump, the goat got to the road that wound round and round the mountain.

"I'll jump up the road," said the goat. "It'll be easy." And it was. Round and round and round the mountain jumped the goat. He really was going up! How proud of himself he was!

"When I get down, the town will be so proud of me," he said. "I'll get a crown. They'll shower me with flowers. How grand I am!"

From sunup to sundown, round and round the mountain jumped the goat. And from sunup to sundown, he didn't stop boasting. From the town to the mountaintop, he jumped and boasted.

And he got there! Up, up, up, where no one in the town could go—up where the clouds were floating.

How proud the goat was now! His mouth and his throat were very dry. But still he shouted loudly, "I am the BEST!"

"I can outcount, outplow, and outpick anyone. I can outjump anyone. I can jump up the mountain. I can outdo anyone at anything," he shouted. "Yes, I am the best!"

On the very top of the very big mountain, he shouted, "I am the best, best, BEST!" Then he grinned his biggest grin and then he bowed his biggest, proudest bow. Leaning way down, he bowed—way, way, WAY down.

And now, in the little town next to the very big mountain, there is no boastful goat.

__ aw __	
law	lawn
paw	yawn
saw	drawn
claw	■
draw	crawl
straw	shawl
■	■
hawk	awful

__ au __	
Paul	August
■	
fault	

__ oi __	
boil	joint
soil	point
toil	■
broil	poison
spoil	
oil	

__ oy
boy
joy
Roy
toy

__ie, __ies, __ied			
die	lie	pie	tie
■	■	■	■
dies	lies	pies	ties
■	■		■
died	lied		tied

__y, __ies, __ied				
cry	dry	fry	fly	try
cries	dries	fries	flies	tries
■	■	■		■
cried	dried	fried		tried

Found on Hawk Mountain

The Sawyers were spending August in the mountains. Mr. and Mrs. Sawyer had visited the mountains in the past. But Paul and Joan hadn't. And they didn't know if it would be fun or not.

Paul and Joan were playing by the stream when they saw some hawks in the sky.

"They must be from Hawk Mountain," said Paul. "You know, Howard's grandfather said there may be hundreds of dollars hidden on Hawk Mountain. He said that when he was a boy some outlaws hid bags of silver coins up there. And nobody has ever found them."

"Paul," Joan said, "wouldn't it be something if we found that silver? Let's try! What do you say?"

"That sounds O.K. Let's go!" said Paul. They left the stream and went up the path to Hawk Mountain.

They were still at the bottom of the mountain when Paul suddenly left the path. He crawled under some stubby trees.

"Come here, Joan. I think I've found something," he said.

He held a chain that was stuck in the ground. He dug just under the soil and found the end of the chain. It was tied to a big chest! He quickly brushed the soil off the lid.

"Wow!" cried Joan. "Lift the lid. I bet we found the silver!"

But the chest was filled with rusty pots and pans.

"O, well. Let's go on," said Joan. "If you were an outlaw, where would you put that silver?"

"I don't know," said Paul. But just then he saw the cliff. "Let's try up there."

Somehow they found a way up the cliff. At the top they saw lots of big rocks and what seemed to be a hawk's nest—but not one silver coin.

"Let's go back," said Joan sadly. "We aren't having any luck, and the sun's going down."

Then, suddenly, they saw something fly by. There was another, and another!

"What's that?" cried Joan.

"They're bats," cried Paul, "and they're coming from that tunnel in the rocks."

The children ran to the tunnel and crawled in. They found that they could stand up. "It's as big as a room in here," said Paul.

They could see a little in the gloom.

"Maybe this is where the outlaws hid the silver," Paul said. And he began to hunt. Joan hunted too.

"Paul, come and see what I've found," she said at last.

"The silver?" cried Paul.

"No. It's just some rocks. But they're chipped in a funny way. Do you see?"

Paul saw some little rocks and some bigger ones. Some were pointed and some were round. But Paul could tell that they weren't just hunks of rock. Someone had neatly chipped each one.

Then he saw the painted clay pot. He picked it up and something in it rattled.

"Silver coins?" asked Joan.

"Maybe," Paul said. The pot was stopped up with dried mud. He had to dig and chip at the mud to get it out. Then he dumped the jug. And out clattered—dried beans!

"Boy!" said Paul. "Beans! And a bunch of rocks. Just what we need!"

"Not a silver coin anywhere," Joan said sadly. "Let's get out of this spooky tunnel."

"O.K. We've got to get back. Do you think Mom and Dad'll want to see this stuff?"

"Maybe," said Joan. She picked up the clay pot and some of the beans. Paul put some of the rocks in his pocket.

Paul and Joan didn't think much of what they had found. But Mr. and Mrs. Sawyer were eager to know everything.

"Where did you say you found them?"

"You say it was way back in a tunnel? In a spot as big as a room?"

"Why, Dad?" asked Paul. "They're just rocks and a pot and some dried beans."

"They're not just rocks," said Mr. Sawyer. "They're flint tools. I think the tools and the pot were left by someone in days past—someone who dressed in skins and hunted beasts to eat."

"I think Dr. Powers should see the tools and the pot," said Mrs. Sawyer. "She spends every August here, hunting for just such tools. She'll know if that's what you've found."

And Dr. Powers did know. She was joyful when she saw what Paul and Joan had found.

"What luck!" she said. "I've hunted in the mountains for the last six summers. But I've never found this many things."

Paul and Joan began to feel happy. But they were puzzled, too.

"What'll we do with them?" Paul asked.

"If it's O.K. with you, I'll send them to Austin, where I teach," said Dr. Powers. "We will want to study them. We have found out a lot from studying such things. That's how we know what went on in the past. And the tools you've found will tell us a lot."

"Really!" said Joan.

"Then," said Dr. Powers, "someday they'll go into a glass box for everyone to see. And the tag on the box will say—

FOUND ON HAWK MOUNTAIN

BY PAUL AND JOAN SAWYER

Paul and Joan grinned. Suddenly the tools and the pot seemed better than outlaws' silver.

Paul and Joan spent the rest of August helping Dr. Powers hunt for other tools. And Mr. and Mrs. Sawyer said that next August they would go to Austin. There they would see the tools, the clay pot, and the dried beans that were—

O Boy – Pie!

I saw two flies
Sit on my pie.
"Get off my pie,
You flies," I cried.

"You spoiled my pie,"
I pointed out,
Trying awfully
Not to shout.

"You spoiled my pie.
I saw you too.
It was MY pie,
And not for you.

"Get off my pie.
Fly to the skies.
Flies go in skies
And not on pies."

The Beaver and the Peacock

One day at the zoo, the peacock asked the beaver, "Why are you so ugly?"

The beaver said he didn't know.

"I know why," said the peacock. "Your teeth are too big and your tail is too flat. How can you be proud of such a tail? Now THIS is something to be proud of."

The peacock ruffled his tail.

"Feel it," he said. "But don't soil it with your paws. It seems to be satin or velvet, doesn't it? Anyway, it's a much better tail than yours."

"Well, that's the last straw!" said the beaver. And he crawled into his den to lie down. "There should be a law to keep peacocks from boasting so much."

Many children in the kingdom went to the zoo to see the peacock. The proud peacock puffed out his chest and fanned his tail. The green in it seemed to shimmer and gleam.

"What a tail the peacock has!" said the children.

One day the queen said that she would visit the town. She was coming on Sunday, and she wanted to visit the zoo.

The town felt proud that the queen was going to pay a royal visit. They cleaned the streets. Then they got dressed up. Fathers put on straw hats, and mothers put on bonnets.

"My!" the peacock said to the beaver. "The queen herself is coming to see my tail. But there's no point in your cleaning up or coming out of your den. She won't want to see you. You're so ugly."

The beaver crawled back into his den.

Soon it was Sunday – the day of the queen's visit. Grandmothers and grandfathers, mothers and fathers, children and pets gathered to see the queen and to welcome her. It was a joyful day.

The mayor of the town welcomed the queen and said, "Here, my queen, is a present for you. It is a painting for your sitting room."

But just as the queen was saying thank you, someone galloped up.

"The river has risen," he yelled. "The dam is cracking. Run for the mountains as fast as you can." Then he galloped off.

The oxen were hitched to wagons. Then mothers and fathers and children got into the wagons. With a crack of the whip, they were off. They went as fast as they could go.

The peacock ran faster than anybody. "This is awful!" he screamed. "I can't swim. What will I do?"

The queen saw what was happening, but no one stopped to help her. "I'll be drowned if no one stops to help me," she sobbed. Still no one stopped.

But the beaver didn't run. "Someone must help the queen," he said. "I have to think of a way to help her!"

The beaver was too little to drag a wagon with the queen in it. And he was too little to pick her up and run with her. What could he do? He tried to think.

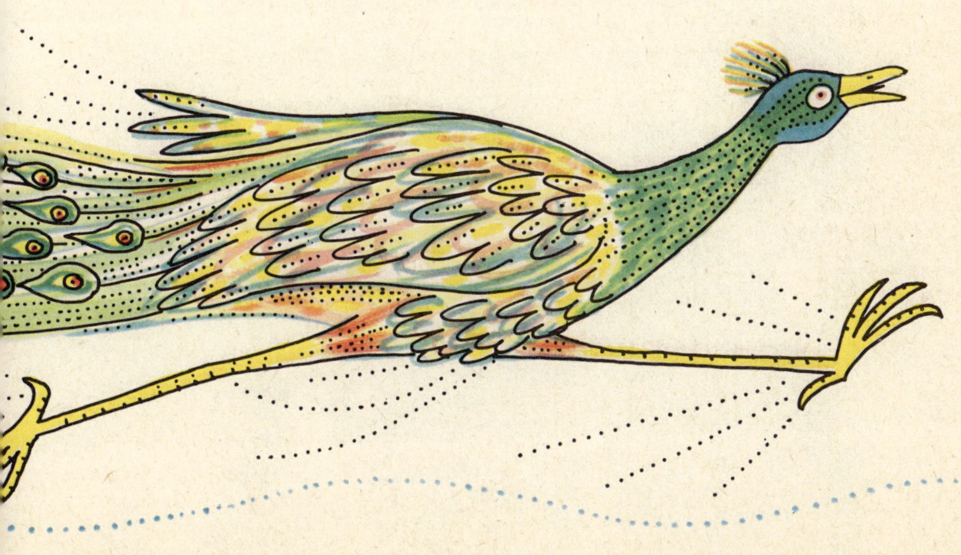

"There's a crack in the dam!" he yelled. "And I know how to fix it!" He quickly cut some logs and twigs with his teeth. Then he lugged them in his mouth to the dam. He stuffed the logs and twigs into the crack with his paws. He patted and stamped and beat them in. Then he put mud on them. And with his big flat tail, he pounded the mud into the crack.

"That does it!" said the beaver at last. "The crack is fixed. The queen won't drown now."

When she saw what the beaver had done, the queen was joyful. "An awful thing could have happened," she said. "But now no one will drown. And we can thank the beaver.

"Beaver," said the queen, "come here."

"I can't," said the beaver. "I'm too ugly to be seen by a queen."

"Yes," said the peacock, who had just come back, "the beaver is too ugly. Maybe you'd rather see me. I AM something to see!"

"What you seem to be does not matter to me," said the queen. "It's what you do that counts. The beaver has just kept everyone from drowning. But what do you do? You ruffle your big, funny tail.

"However, we do need big, funny tails in this kingdom. We need them to sweep the streets. From now on, you are to sweep the streets with your big, funny tail."

And from that day on, the peacock swept the streets. But the beaver—with his big teeth and flat tail—put up the dams. It was the law of the land.

Uncle Roy

My Uncle Roy's an actor—
A cowboy on TV.
He plays The Hawk each Sunday,
And he's really fun to see.

The Hawk's a western lawman
Who never draws a gun.
He catches men by tricking them,
He traps them one by one.

He tracks down every outlaw,
He spoils each awful plan.
Nobody can fool him,
He's such a tricky man.

He never shoots the outlaws
Or ties up anyone.
He just fools them into jail,
And so his job gets done.

It's really very funny
To see the tricks he tries.
The plays are never sad to see,
And no one ever dies.

He's such a clever actor,
He's really fun to see.
I'm glad I have an uncle
Who's a cowboy on TV.

Tenjin's Day at Sea

Tenjin saw Captain Yashima's fishing boat drawing up to the dock. "Captain," he cried, "how was the catch?"

"The fish were running well, my boy," the captain shouted back. "The hatch is filled with fish!"

Captain Yashima was the proudest captain in the land that day. He had just got his little boat.

It was a little boat, but it ran on gas. His other boat had had a sail and couldn't go as fast. And it couldn't go out to sea when there was no wind.

But he would catch many, many fish with this boat.

Tenjin was proud of Captain Yashima's boat too. He wanted to be a fisherman and have such a boat.

Captain Yashima and his helper tied the boat up to the dock. Tenjin jumped on deck to help them. Each day he helped them get the fish up from the hatch and onto the dock. Then he helped load the fish onto a truck. The truck hauled the fish up the coast where they could be dried or canned.

And each day Captain Yashima let Tenjin have a bucket of fish.

Tenjin didn't help just so he could get a bucket of fish. He wanted the captain to teach him to run the boat.

But whenever he asked, the captain said no.

"You must wait," he would say. "You're just a boy. This is a job for a man."

One day when Tenjin went to the dock, he saw that the captain was still there.

"There won't be any fishing today," Captain Yashima said sadly. "My helper is sick, and I can't fish without a helper."

"Captain, let me go," said Tenjin. "I know I can help. You mustn't miss a day of fishing."

"Tenjin," the captain said, "the Inland Sea seems smooth. But it's not. The boat will rock and tip and you could slip on the deck. I'd think it was my fault if you fell into the sea."

But Tenjin begged and begged. And at last the captain said he could go.

It was a hot August day, and the sailing was smooth. Captain Yashima kept his hand on the wheel. Tenjin stayed next to him and studied how he ran the boat.

When they were out to sea, the captain let out the nets. When the nets were filled with fish, the captain would draw them in. He and Tenjin would dump the fish into the hatch. Then they would cast the nets back into the sea.

Tenjin tried to do just what the captain said. And Captain Yashima was very happy with him.

"You're a big help to me," the captain said. And Tenjin grinned with joy.

But at noon the wind began to rock the boat. The sea seemed to boil. Black clouds began to fill the skies.

"Tenjin, a bad rain's coming. We're going back to the dock!" cried Captain Yashima. But just then the boat tipped. The captain slipped on a spot of oil—and fell into the sea.

Captain Yashima could swim well. He was floating, but he was being swept quickly out to sea.

For a second, Tenjin didn't know what to do. Then he saw an empty gas can. Empty cans float! He grabbed the can and pitched it out to the captain.

"Grab this and hang on to it!" Tenjin cried. "I can run the boat. I'll pick you up!"

Tenjin spun the wheel, and the boat went swinging back. He flipped a switch and the boat stopped next to Captain Yashima.

The boat was rocking badly. But Tenjin held on. He tied one end of a ladder to the boat's railing. He dropped the other end into the sea.

Captain Yashima grabbed the ladder and crawled up. Tenjin helped him onto the deck.

"Lie down and rest," Tenjin said. "I'll bring you a towel and some dry trousers and socks."

The captain was weak. But he did say, "Thank you, Tenjin. If it weren't for your quick thinking, I could have died in the sea."

The captain rested. Then he ran the boat back to the dock. He let Tenjin handle the wheel much of the way.

When the boat was tied up at the dock, the captain counted out Tenjin's fish. Tenjin got the best of the day's catch—so many that he couldn't eat them in a week.

But better than that was what Captain Yashima said: "Tenjin, you may be just a boy, but you've done a man's job today. Someday soon you'll be the best fisherman on the Inland Sea."

__ar
calendar
▪
caterpillar
▪
vinegar

__al
animal
▪
hospital
▪
several

__a
Africa
▪
camera
▪
Canada

__ent
different
▪
president
▪
resident

__y
lullaby
▪
satisfy

__ble
possible
▪
terrible

__y
enemy
▪
family

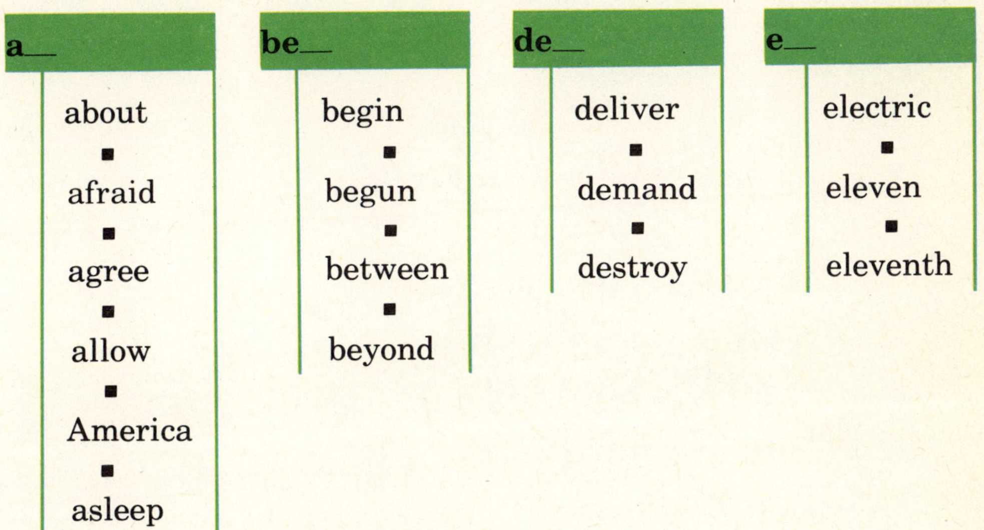
a__
about
afraid
agree
allow
America
asleep
be__
begin
begun
between
beyond
de__
deliver
demand
destroy
e__
electric
eleven
eleventh

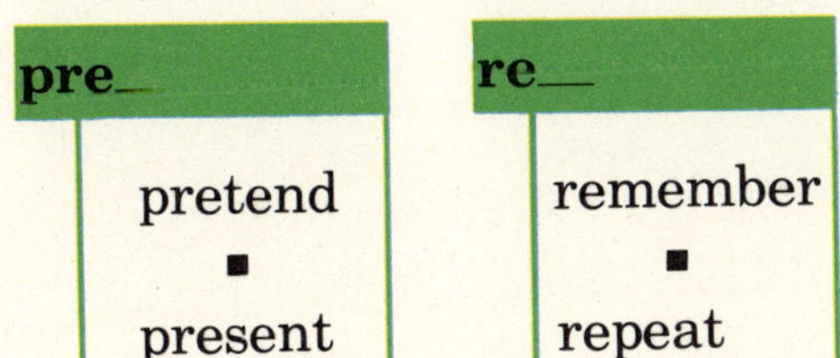
pre__
pretend
present
re__
remember
repeat

Visitor

A telegram
Has come to say
A visitor
Is on his way.
We do expect
A visitor
At two.

I do enjoy
A visitor's visit.
Not a thing's
As much fun – is it?
As a visit
From a visitor
Or two.

I will clean
Beneath my bed,
Exactly as
My mother said.
I'll collect,
Without a sound,
Everything
I've left around.
I'll agree
To dress up neatly
And remember
To speak sweetly.

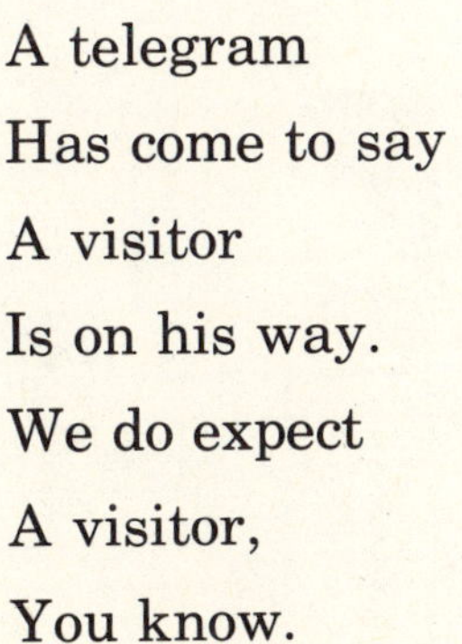

A telegram
Has come to say
A visitor
Is on his way.
We do expect
A visitor,
You know.

I do enjoy
A visitor's visit.
Not a thing's
As much fun – is it?
As a visit
From a visitor
Or so.

When everything
Is said and done,
Having visitors
Is such fun.
It's grand to see
A different someone,
And to get
A greeting
From one.

My Funny Chickadee

When my father sings
  A lullaby to me,
I begin to dream
  About a chickadee.

This funny chickadee
  Pretends he is a man.
He puts on red pajamas
  As quickly as he can.

He has a red umbrella
  When rain has not begun.
He snaps a little camera
  As if he's having fun.

Indeed I go to sleep
  As quickly as I can
To see my chickadee
  Pretending he's a man.

The Back of Beyond

The clock had just struck one when eleven masked men crept into Amanda's bedroom.

They gathered around her bed, whispering.

Amanda ducked underneath the sheet. "I'll pretend the men aren't there," she said to herself. "Maybe they'll go away then."

But they didn't.

"Is she asleep?" asked one.

"I don't think so," said another.

"What about the rest of her family? Are they asleep?"

"They are."

"You checked, did you?"

"Indeed I did."

"You there," demanded one of the men. "We know you're not asleep."

"Maybe she's afraid," said another.

"It's possible. But unless she comes out, how can we deliver the letter?"

"I don't know. This could destroy the plans."

"Indeed it could."

"But we can't allow that. We must get the letter to the president."

"Indeed we must."

Amanda sat up.

"Did you say something about the president?" she asked.

The men stopped whispering, and one of them stepped up to present himself to Amanda.

"That's better," he said. "We had begun to think you were afraid of us. And yes, we did say something about the president."

"But what president do you mean?" asked Amanda. "There are at least several that I know of."

"We mean your president. The president of this land."

Well, that was different.

Amanda was interested now. She was so interested that she didn't remember that she was afraid.

"Who are you?" she asked. "And where have you come from?"

"We have come from the Back of Beyond. And we were sent here by our leader."

"From the Back of Beyond?" said Amanda. Where is that?"

"Well, you could say it's between Africa, Canada, and September."

"That's not too plain," said Amanda. "But tell me, why has your leader sent you?"

"There is something the president must know. We have the facts of the matter, and they must get to the president as soon as possible."

"The facts of what matter?"

"It's spelled out in this letter."

"And what do you want with me?" asked Amanda.

"We have selected you to go to the president to present the facts. But I repeat: you must go as soon as possible."

"Why don't you go?"

"We can't."

"I see," said Amanda. "Well, I'll do it if you say so. Where is the letter?"

"You can't have the letter. We will tell you what is in it, and after that it must be destroyed."

"Why is that?"

"So it won't get into the hands of the enemy."

"I understand," said Amanda.

The man slipped the letter from his pocket and leaned down to read it to Amanda.

He began to read in a whisper, and a chill went up Amanda's back.

"Why, that's terrible," said Amanda.

The man nodded.

"It is indeed," he said. "So you must go to the president and ask for help as soon as the sun comes up. And remember that we're counting on you."

"I will."

"There's just one thing . . ."

"Yes?"

"It's possible you won't remember what the letter said."

"But I will. How could I help but remember?"

"Well, if you must know, we have asked others to go to the president for us. Many others. And they said that they would. But not one of them has remembered."

"Trust me," said Amanda. "I'll remember." And she repeated what the letter had said.

The eleven men crept from the bedroom, and Amanda lay back to wait for the sun.

As soon as it was up, she leaped from her bed.

She got out of her pajamas, dressed herself, and rushed from the bedroom.

She ran down the steps.

The rest of her family was up too.

"Amanda," said her mother, "where are you going?"

Amanda stopped at the bottom of the steps.

She blinked at her mother.

"What is it?" her mother asked. "Don't you feel well?"

Amanda's mouth fell.

"The letter," she said. "I can't remember what it said."

Try as she would, she could not remember.

To this day, she can't remember.

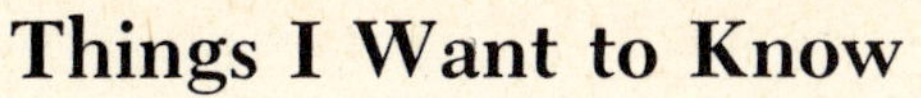

Things I Want to Know

Do train conductors ever rest?
  Do caterpillars dream?
Is there a king of Canada?
  Does buttermilk have cream?

Who delivers telegrams?
  Do expressways have an end?
Who enjoys the hospitals?
  How does Mom's umbrella bend?

Are pajamas just for sleep?
  Do electric trains have teas?
Do fish enjoy lullabies?
  Do bananas come from trees?

I've interest in so many things!
  That's why I'm asking you.
I stop to think about each one.
  I know that you do too.

The Caterpillar Who Sang Lullabies

In a little town there was a caterpillar who sang better than any other caterpillar around. In fact, not one animal between there and Africa could sing as well.

"I'm the best singer around," said the caterpillar. He repeated that boast after each lullaby. He didn't know it, but he didn't sing anything BUT lullabies.

One day a dog complained to the caterpillar, "I'm unhappy. I can't sleep. Will you sing me a lullaby?"

The caterpillar was underneath a banana tree, eating bananas. "Yes," he said, "I'll do it."

The caterpillar stopped eating and sang. And soon the dog was fast asleep.

The next day a chickadee hopped up to the banana tree. The dog was still sleeping beneath the tree, in a bed of flowers.

"Did you put that terrier to sleep?" the chickadee asked the caterpillar. He yawned as he said it.

"I'll say I did," bragged the caterpillar.

"Then how about me?" demanded the chickadee. "Put me to sleep too."

"Indeed I will," said the caterpillar, and he sang his lullaby. The chickadee fell asleep in the flowers with the terrier.

Next an owl landed in the banana tree. "Allow me to ask you something," he said.

"Ask," said the caterpillar.

"Can you sing me to sleep?"

"Anything is possible," said the caterpillar. And he sang. Faster than you can blink, the owl fell asleep.

Now if an owl can be put to sleep, that's something. Soon animals from everywhere were coming to see the lullaby-singing caterpillar. There were hawks, and goats, and toads, and snails—and a rooster who had come by express train from Canada. He had his pajamas in a little bag.

"Put us to sleep," the animals demanded. So the caterpillar did. Soon every bit of ground around the banana tree was filled with sleeping animals.

And other animals kept coming every day. They wanted to be sung to sleep too. But the caterpillar had to send them away disappointed. "Sorry," he'd say, "but there just isn't any room."

And the caterpillar began to get sick of it. "Sleeping toads here! Sleeping goats there! They've trampled the grass and crushed the flowers. I've got to get them up and out of here!" he complained.

But he didn't know how.

He tried singing, but the animals didn't get up. They just slept on.

The caterpillar went to the hospital for help. Eleven doctors went to see the sleeping animals. But the eleven doctors just said, "We don't know how to stop them from sleeping."

"This is terrible. This is terrible," said the unhappy caterpillar.

September passed, and it was getting chilly. But the animals still slept in the flowers underneath the banana tree.

Then one day an Indian passed by on a green cow. He saw the animals asleep and stopped. "What's this?" asked the Indian. The green cow began to eat the flowers under the banana tree.

"I sang the animals a lullaby," said the caterpillar. "It put them to sleep. And they just go on sleeping! I'm sick of them and I want to get rid of them. But now it's impossible to get them up."

"Indeed," said the Indian. "How did you go about it?"

"Go about what?" said the caterpillar. "Putting them to sleep or getting them up?"

"Getting them up," said the Indian.

"I sang to them," said the caterpillar.

"Well," said the Indian, "let's try something different."

"What?" asked the caterpillar.

"This," said the Indian. He put his hands to his mouth and yelled, "DINNER!"

"Let's go eat," he yelled. "Let's go EAT! Everybody get up for DINNER – Thanksgiving dinner! LET'S GO EAT! DIN-DIN-DINNER!"

Suddenly every animal – the dogs, chickadees, owls, hawks, goats, toads, snails, and the rooster from Canada – jumped up and cried out together, "WHERE?"

The Indian pointed down the road, and the animals began running. Each one ran back to where he could get some dinner.

When no animals remained, the Indian got back on his green cow. "We have to catch a train," he said. And he left.

The caterpillar painted

NO SINGING!

on the banana tree. Then he sat down to enjoy being by himself.

Casper Caterpillar

Casper Caterpillar cried.
He wished to go to sea.
"Don't go, my boy," his father said.
"Stay with the family."

But when his family fell asleep,
Bad Casper slipped away.
He crawled upon a boat of weeds
And sailed that very day.

"I'm off for Africa!" he cried.
"I don't think I can miss it.
I don't remember where it is,
But that's the spot I'll visit."

Just then a sudden wind sprang up
And swept his boat about.
"Alas!" unhappy Casper cried,
"I shouldn't have come out!"

The wind was terrible indeed,
And Casper was afraid.
"What will become of me?" he wept,
"I wish I'd never strayed."

As Casper cried in deep distress,
A gull was flying by.
He spied unlucky Casper
And attacked him from the sky!

The weeds in Casper's little boat
Were every tint of green,
So he could crawl beneath them
And shiver there unseen.

"Your skin is green," the gull complained,
"Impossible to see,
And you are slippery and wet.
Don't run away from me!"

But Casper didn't want to be
A greedy seagull's dinner.
He stayed within the weeds and said,
"I wish that I were thinner!"

The gull sped off, the wind died down,
But Casper still was wailing.
He had no interest in his boat,
In Africa, or sailing.

"I want my family," he cried,
"I do NOT want the sea!"
And so he went back to his nest
And stayed there happily.

__a__e					
	date	bake	came	made	cape
	gate	cake	game	blade	grape
	hate	lake	name	grade	shape
	late	make	same	shade	scrape
	skate	take	blame	trade	escape
	plate	flake	flame	parade	ape
	ate	shake	became	lemonade	■
	■	awake			chase
	cave	mistake			■
	gave				taste
	save				
	wave				
	forgave				

__i__e

fine	dime	hide	bite	file
line	time	ride	kite	mile
mine	■ five	slide	quite	pile
nine	hive	beside	white	smile
vine	drive	divide	invite	awhile
shine	alive	inside	polite	
valentine	arrive		■ bike	

__o__e

joke	bone	hose	hole	drove
woke	cone	nose	pole	stove
broke	shone	rose	stole	
smoke	stone	chose	■ note	
spoke	throne	close	vote	
awoke	alone	those	■ home	
		suppose		

__u__e

rude	use
crude	excuse
include	■ cube
■ June	tube
tune	
■ rule	

__e__e

Pete	Steve
complete	eve
concrete	■ these

The Greedy Ape

An ape went up a banana tree
And ate some bananas—twenty-three!
It got so big and fat, you see,
It couldn't get back down the tree.

Here's a rule you should remember,
Here's a rule that you should prize:
Eating way too much at mealtime
Isn't ever, ever wise.

You may want a lot of jelly,
And you may want too much cake,
But too much of anything
Can be a big mistake.

Sam the Rainmaker

Way out West, there was an Indian town by the name of East Snakeskin. And in the town was an Indian rainmaker by the name of Sam. The Indians in East Snakeskin were very proud of Sam. He was the best rainmaker in the West. They used to say, "If anyone can make it rain, Sam can."

Sam had nineteen prizes for making it rain. There weren't any other prizes, or Sam would have had them too.

Thanks to Sam, East Snakeskin was the one town in the West where every Indian had an umbrella. He made it rain so much that the Indians couldn't plant grain when the time came. It was too wet.

So they went to Sam and said, "How about NOT making it rain for a while, Sam? How about some sunshine—some fine, HOT sunshine? How about it, Sam?"

Well, that made Sam mad. It was his job to make rain. Besides, he LIKED to make rain. And he didn't see why the Indians couldn't just plant the grain in the rain. They had umbrellas. But Sam didn't say that aloud.

He just became very polite and said, "My mistake. It seemed to me I was SUPPOSED to make it rain. It seemed to me that was my job. My mistake. So sorry. Do excuse me."

The Indian leader said, "Now, Sam, don't take it like that." But Sam just went inside, and he didn't invite anyone to come in with him. So the other Indians went away and waited for the rain to stop and the sun to shine. In just a little while, it did.

The Indians went out and planted the grain. Sam sat around and napped a lot. It didn't rain, and the sun kept on shining. Day after day, the sun blazed away. After being the wettest town in the West, East Snakeskin became the driest. Well, grain needs rain, so the grain didn't ripen. And the Indians were running out of food.

The Indian leader said, "We need rain for the grain. How about asking Sam to do a little rainmaking?" But nobody wanted to ask him. Everybody in East Snakeskin paraded around town with closed umbrellas. They hoped Sam would see them and make it rain. But he didn't. He was inside, taking a nap in his red bathrobe.

At last the leader went up to Sam's home and yelled, "Wake up, Sam! Time to make it rain! We're running out of food, and we need rain for the grain."

"O, you do, do you?" Sam said. "Last time it was how about NOT making it rain? How about a little sunshine? Well, the sun's shining."

"Now, Sam," said the Indian leader, "don't take it like that. Sometimes we need sun and sometimes we need rain. Now we need rain. And if anyone can make it rain, you can. Besides, it's your job."

"Yes," the other Indians said. "If anyone can make it rain, you can, Sam."

So Sam went inside. He put on his rainmaking outfit—a red-and-white-striped cape. Then he came out and lit a fire. He got a big kettle and put it on the flames. He dropped a lot of stuff into the kettle. When the stuff in the kettle boiled up, Sam sang a rain chant.

The other Indians ran to get umbrellas. They said, "If anyone can make it rain, Sam can. He will make it rain for the grain."

In no time there was a big cloud in the sky, and it began to thunder. And then it rained. But no one got wet. It rained big ripe pineapples. The Indians had to put up the umbrellas to keep from getting banged by the pineapples.

The Indian leader said, "Well, we have no rain for the grain, so we'll have to eat pineapples." So the Indians ate pineapples.

About eleven days later, the pineapples were finished. The Indian leader went back to Sam. Sam was taking another nap.

"Wake up, Sam!" he yelled. "Time to make it rain. We need rain for the grain."

"What's the matter?" Sam asked. "Don't you like pineapples?"

"Pineapples are fine, but we finished them," the Indian leader said. "And some of us are getting sick of pineapples. How about some rain for the grain, Sam? If anyone can make it rain, you can."

So Sam put on his rainmaking outfit and came out and lit his fire. The other Indians ran for umbrellas and raincoats. Then he sang a rain chant. In no time there was a big cloud in the sky and it began to thunder. Then it began to rain.

But nobody got wet. And it didn't rain pineapples. As a matter of fact, it rained cakes. It rained cupcakes, pancakes, and pineapple upside-down cakes. (There must have been some pineapples left in the cloud.) The Indians put up umbrellas, but in no time they were waist-deep in cakes.

So the Indian leader said, "Well, there's no rain for the grain, so we'll have to eat cake."

About eleven days later, the cake was finished. By now, the Indian leader was quite unhappy. It was time to wake up Sam.

"Wake up, Sam!" the leader yelled. "Time to make it rain. And, Sam – a joke's a joke, but quit the clowning, will you? We need rain for the grain."

"Who's clowning?" Sam asked. "What's the matter? Don't you like cake?"

"The cake is finished," said the Indian leader. "Besides, some of us are getting sick of cake. How about some rain for the grain?"

So Sam went out and lit his fire. When he put stuff into his kettle, some of the Indians went to get umbrellas, but some didn't. Some just went inside. Sam waited for them to say, "If anyone can make it rain, Sam can."

Nobody said it. Sam began to sing his rain chant. Then he stopped. "How about some frozen banana goo?" he asked.

"Sam," said the Indian leader, "what we need is rain for the grain. And what we WANT is rain for the grain." And he added, "Some of us are beginning to think you've forgotten how to make it rain."

"O, is that so?" said Sam. He poked up his fire and sang his rain chant.

In no time there was a big cloud in the sky, and it began to thunder. It began to rain. This time it was REAL rain. The Indians who were inside came out and put up umbrellas. Everybody said, "See? If anyone can make it rain, Sam can." And the rain was fine for the grain.

But one little boy said, "I LIKE cake. And I LIKE pineapple. And I think I'd like frozen banana goo. Why should Sam make it rain RAIN every time? When we don't need rain, why don't we ask Sam to make it rain something different?"

The other Indians agreed. So now East Snakeskin is the one town in the West where it sometimes rains rain, and sometimes grape milkshakes or lemon-cream pies. One time it rained cowboys. But that's another tale.

A Fishy Tale

I woke at sunrise.
  "Rise and shine,"
My father said.
  "Today is fine."

I saw a pole.
  I was awake.
Today we'd fish
  In Brave Man's Lake.

The sun shone hot.
  And then at nine
I felt a tug
  Upon my line.

"A strike!" I yelled.
  "He's quite a size."
"Hang on," said Dad.
  "That fish is wise."

My feet and hands
  Began to slide.
My father stayed there
  By my side.

"He feels as big
  As a whale would be.
Suppose he gets
  Away from me?"

My father smiled.
  "That's just your tale –
Don't be afraid.
  He's not a whale."

"Well, maybe not.
  But with his size,
I think he'll win me
  Quite a prize."

And then the pole
  Began to shake,
And Father said,
  "It's some mistake."

We saw the fish
  And Dad was pale,
For on my line
  Was one white whale.

"A whale! A whale!
  MY whale!" I said.
And then I woke up

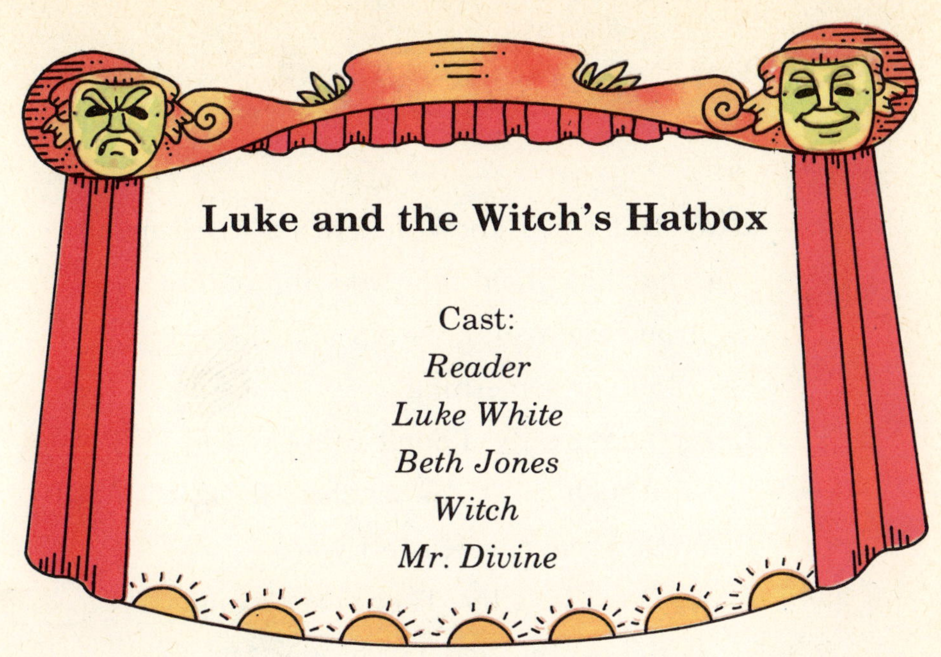

Luke and the Witch's Hatbox

Cast:
Reader
Luke White
Beth Jones
Witch
Mr. Divine

Act 1

Reader: It was lunchtime on a weekend day. Luke White was late for lunch. He and his pal Beth Jones had to stop playing, and Luke had to go home.

Luke: See you later, Beth. I have to go home now. I'll go past the empty lot to Balantine Street. It's quicker that way.

Beth: Don't go past that lot, Luke!

Luke: Why not?

Beth: Don't you know? There's a witch in that lot! She'll take you and make you into a snake or an ape or a stone or something!

Luke: That's silly. I don't think there are such things as witches, Beth.

Beth: Don't go there, I tell you!

Luke: Don't be silly. There aren't any witches. Besides, I'm brave. And I have to go now. See you later.

Beth: It's not safe! You'll see!

Reader: But despite what Beth said, Luke went past the empty lot. There was a stick in his way. Luke kicked the stick. And when he did, there was a cry.

Witch: Ouch!

Luke: Who said that?

Witch: I did. Pick me up.

Reader: It was the stick that spoke! Now Luke was brave, but not very wise. So he bent down to pick up the stick that spoke. Boom! Poof! There was smoke and fire and flame. When the smoke went away, there was an ugly witch standing beside Luke! The ugly witch had claws on her feet. She had on a black cape and an ugly hat. The hat had twelve sides.

Witch: Now I've got you! You shouldn't have picked up that stick, for it was not really a stick. It was ME in the shape of a stick. And when you did what I said to do—when you picked it up—you put yourself in my power. Those are the rules:

DO WHAT A WITCH TELLS YOU TO DO,
AND SHE WILL GET HER CLAWS IN YOU.

Ho, ho! Hee, hee, hee!

Reader: Luke didn't feel brave now. He went pale and began to shake. He could see that he had made a mistake. He wanted to escape.

Luke: Wh-what are you going to do to me?

Witch: I'm going to punish you for kicking me.

Luke: I'm sorry about that. I didn't know it was you. I just saw a stick.

Witch: That's your problem—not mine, Luke White. (Yes, I know your name.) Now you have to pay. I'm going to make YOU into a stick so children can kick you and ride bikes on top of you. Boys will pitch you and dogs will fetch you and bite you. Hee, hee, hee!

Luke: Would you really do that to me?

Witch: You bet I would, unless . . .

Luke: Unless what?

Witch: Unless you would like to do a task for me.

Reader: How could Luke refuse? His life was at stake.

Luke: Yes! I'll do anything you like if you'll let me alone. Just don't make me into a stick. I'll do what you like if I can save my life that way.

Witch: You see my ugly hat with its twelve sides?

Luke: Yes it is – I mean, yes I do.

Witch: I need a box for it. And I can't get one. You must get me a twelve-sided box for my twelve-sided hat.

Luke: I'll try! But I've never seen a twelve-sided box. It won't be easy to get one.

Witch: That's your problem – not mine. You have just one day. If you aren't back here in one day with a twelve-sided box, you will become a stick – wherever you are!

Reader: Boom! Poof! There was another cloud of smoke and fire and flame. The ugly witch vanished, and Luke was left alone.

ACT 2

Reader: Bad luck for Luke! Where could he get a twelve-sided box in just one day? He went to the shops close by. But no one had such a box. No one had ever seen such a box. Then Mr. Divine, the man at the food shop, asked Luke why he wanted the box.

Mr. Divine: Why do you want such a funny box, Luke?

Luke: I said I'd get it for the ugly witch in the empty lot between Balantine Street and Stevens Road. If I fail, she'll make me into a stick! Can't you help me, Mr. Divine?

Mr. Divine: Is this a joke?

Reader: It wasn't easy, but after a while Luke made Mr. Divine see that he was really in a bad fix. And Mr. Divine agreed to help.

Mr. Divine: I don't have a twelve-sided box, Luke. But I have this plain box. And I have a plan. I hope it will do the trick.

Reader: Mr. Divine put the plain box in a big sack and gave it to Luke. Then he said something to Luke. Then Luke left.

Luke: Thanks, Mr. Divine!

Mr. Divine: Lots of luck, Luke!

ACT 3

Reader: Luke went back to the lot between Balantine Street and Stevens Road to meet the ugly witch. He yelled out bravely—

Luke: UGLY WITCH! I AM BACK!
I HAVE YOUR BOX IN THIS BIG SACK!

Reader: Boom! Poof! Smoke, fire, and flame! Up popped the ugly witch!

Witch: Let's see the box!

Luke: If it's really twelve-sided, will you let me alone?

Witch: That's the deal.

Reader: Luke poked his hand into the sack and got out the box.

Witch: What! That's just a plain 4-sided box! You've failed! Now you're going to get it:

HICKERY-DICKERY-DICK
LUKE WHITE BECOMES A . . .

Luke: Wait! Stop! You're forgetting something. It has a top side and a bottom side too. Add those in.

Witch: So what! That's still just six. You've had it, kid!

HICKERY-DICKERY-DICK . . .

Luke: Wait! I haven't finished yet!

Reader: Luke lifted the lid off the box. He held it so the ugly witch could see inside.

Luke: What do you see here?

Witch: Not a thing. It's empty.

Luke: But don't you see? There are six INSIDE sides to go with the six outside sides. What's six and six? Isn't it twelve?

Witch: What trick is this? My ugly hat won't fit in that box!

Luke: That's your problem—not mine. You got what you asked for. I got you a twelve-sided box. Now you have to keep your end of the deal. You have to let me alone as you said you would.

Reader: O, that ugly witch was mad! But what Luke said was so. Witches have to keep the deals they make. And Luke HAD got her a box with twelve sides. So the ugly witch couldn't do anything to Luke. She just went Boom! Poof! And in a cloud of smoke and fire and flame she vanished.

Luke: It's a shame she left so fast. I wanted to tell her what to ask for next time. A 28-sided box would be just fine for her ugly hat.

Reader: What Luke said was so. A 28-sided box would be just fine for the ugly witch's ugly twelve-sided hat. And do you know why? If not, that's your problem – not mine!

I'm Afraid I'm Not Brave

If a bee invited
  Me inside
Its little hive,
  I'd have to hide.

If a snake politely
  Said, "Let's shake,"
I'd say, "Excuse me,
  My mistake."

If an ape chased me
  Just to say,
"Be my playmate
  For today,"
I'm afraid
  I would not smile,
And possibly
  Would run a mile.

Trapped in a Cave

Jones's cave was a mile outside of Appleton, Dave's home town. The mouth of the cave was on the side of a hill on Mr. Jones's ranch. The children of Appleton played there. The mothers and fathers weren't very happy about it. They were afraid it wasn't safe. But the children weren't afraid, and they went there many times.

One day, when Dave was on the side of the hill, he yelled to his playmates, "I've found another hole. It's so big I can't see the end of it!"

Emily and Steve ran up to see.

"Where do you suppose this leads?" Dave asked. "Could it be another way to get into Jones's cave?"

"Let's tie a rope around Dave," said Emily. "Then he can go into the hole and see."

Everyone agreed. Dave crawled into the hole and down about twenty-five feet. Soon he shouted up, "Tie the rope to a tree and come on in. There's a big room down here. It must be a room of Jones's cave that we never found in the past."

So Emily and Steve went into the hole. It was the best room they had ever seen in the cave.

"We've found a way into the cave that nobody knows about," said Emily.

"And nobody knows about this room," said Steve. "Why don't we have a club? We'll name it the Cave Club, and this can be the meeting room."

"Swell!" said Dave. Dave had found the room, so he was made president of the club.

Then Steve said, "I think we should have a rule that no one can tell anyone about the club or the clubroom."

The children agreed, and they voted for the rule.

Each day after that, the children met in the cave. Sometimes they would take food from home and have lunch there.

One Sunday afternoon, Dave saw everyone from Appleton going out to Jones's cave. Dave stopped one of them. "Mr. Chase, has anything happened?"

"There was a big rockslide out at Jones's hill," Mr. Chase explained. "The way into the cave is blocked. Mr. White's children, Pete and Sally, are inside. We're trying to get them out."

Dave ran to get Emily and Steve. When they arrived at the cave, men were digging in a pile of stones, trying to get inside.

"Come on," said Dave. "We've got to have a club meeting. We've got to vote on the rule about not telling about the clubroom."

"But if we tell," said Steve, "my mom and dad will be mad. So will yours. They won't let us come here, and we won't have a clubroom."

"I know it," said Dave. "But we've got to help get Sally and Pete out. We don't know how much time it may take to dig into the cave."

They had a quick meeting and voted to tell the men about the hidden way into the cave. Then they explained to Mr. Chase.

"But there can't be another way in," said one man. "I'm from around here, and I've never seen one. Now you children run off and play. We've got digging to do."

But Mr. White, who was Pete and Sally's father, wanted to see. The children pointed out the hole. Several men went down on ropes. And there they found Pete and Sally White, alive and safe.

"Are we glad to see you!" said Pete. "We didn't know there was another way to get out."

"Nobody did," said Emily. "Nobody but us."

"And now you know where our clubroom is," said Dave, grinning. "We'll have to make you members."

"But you can't have club meetings in this cave," said Mr. White. "I don't want you coming up here alone. You see what can happen."

The children agreed. But they weren't happy.

"It was such a neat clubroom," said Emily.

"And we don't have another room to meet in," said Steve.

"I'll tell you what," said Mr. White. "I'm so glad to have Sally and Pete safe – and I'm so grateful to you for your help – that I'll get you a clubroom."

Mr. White had a big shed way back in the hills. He cleaned it and fixed it up and gave it to the club. And just members of the Cave Club could go there.

The King's Present

A blacksmith was making a present for the king. "I'll make him some fine lamps," he said to his wife.

"No," said the blacksmith's wife. "You gave him lamps the last time. Make something different."

The blacksmith smiled. "I suppose I could make him a fine brass bathtub."

"I think he'd like that," said the wife.

So the blacksmith began. He fanned the fire, and soon it was blazing. BANG-BANG-BANG went his hammer. Soon the tub was shaped. Then he rubbed it with a rag, inside and outside. He rubbed it until it was shiny.

"What a fine, shiny brass bathtub," said the smith's wife. "Let's take it to the king."

The blacksmith agreed. He tipped the tub upside down and got inside. Then he lifted it up and his wife led him. Soon children began to skip after them. The silly parade made everyone smile.

"Where are you taking that bathtub?" asked the children.

"It's a gift for the king," said the smith's wife.

"The blacksmith thinks the king smells!" shouted the children. "The smith thinks the king needs a bath!"

"Stop! Stop that!" the blacksmith yelled. But the children wouldn't stop.

The smith and his wife were afraid.

"Suppose these children shouted that to the king," he said. "The king won't like it. And who will he blame? Us. What a mistake we have made."

"We had better escape while we can," said his wife.

So they struggled up the hillside, dragging the tub after them.

In the meantime, the children were playing outside the throne room. "The blacksmith thinks the king smells!" they shouted.

The king awoke from a nap he was taking. "Go home!" he shouted to the children. "You are rude and impolite to make jokes about the king!"

"We're not joking," the children said. "The blacksmith made you a brass bathtub. Would he do that if he didn't think you needed a bath?"

"O he did, did he?" said the king. "Where is he?"

"He ran up the hillside to hide," said the children.

The king shouted for his men. They rode down the street and out the gate, and thundered up the hillside.

Somehow the smith had dragged the tub to the very top. When he got there he was hot and sticky.

"I see no reason to waste this fine bathtub," he said. "I'll take a bath."

His wife filled the tub from a spring close by. Then he undressed and got in the tub. Splash-splash-splash.

"I feel a little better," he said. "But I wish I had some soap. I'm still sticky. I don't feel completely clean."

His wife began to shake. "I hope you don't want me to go home for some."

"Thanks for offering," said the smith.

She went down one path as the king came up another. Up and up he came—closer and closer. Suddenly he saw the smith in the bathtub.

"Take him alive!" cried the king.

But the blacksmith held his nose and ducked under. That made the tub slip, and it began to slide down the hill. It slid like a sled – BUMP-BUMP-BUMP! The smith sat up and saw a cliff.

"Catch him!" cried the king. "Don't let him escape! Don't let the tub slide off the cliff!"

The blacksmith agreed. "Catch me!" he cried. "Catch me!"

The king's men tried to grab the tub but they missed. It zoomed off the cliff. Down and down it tumbled until – kerplash! – it landed in a little pond.

"Fine," said the king. "He'll drown when that brass bathtub sinks!"

But it didn't sink. A metal bathtub doesn't sink.

This made the king very unhappy. "Dive in and get him!" he shouted. "Don't let him escape. I'll teach him to make bathtubs for kings!"

The king's men dove into the pond and got around the tub.

The blacksmith tried to smile.

"Bathtub?" he asked bravely. "What bathtub? This is a brass boat. My, but I'm having fun," he added.

"Boat?" said the king. "It was described to me as a bathtub."

"How silly," said the smith. "You can see for yourself it's a boat."

"And I suppose you'll say you made it for me," said the king.

"Yes, I did," said the smith.

"What a funny way to deliver it," said the king.

"I had to try it out," said the smith. "I'd hate to have it sink if YOU were in it."

"I see," said the king. "Very wise of you. For your sake, I'm glad it's a boat. It would be rude to offer a king a bathtub. And there is no excuse for rudeness to a ruler. Don't you agree?"

"I agree," said the smith.

The king handed the smith a fine silk robe. "Put this on," he said. "You and your wife are invited to supper. We'll eat it in the throne room later. Now I'm going to take a ride in my shiny brass boat."

Just as the smith was about to go home, the king said, "You know what? This boat would make a fine bathtub."

And the king and the blacksmith grinned at each other.

Hide-and-Seek

"Let's play hide-and-seek,"
  Said a snake to an ape,
"And the prize will be
  A yummy ripe grape."

"That's fine," said the ape.
  "I'll count up to five.
You hide yourself,
  Like a bee in a hive."

The snake slid away
  And hid himself deep
Inside an apple,
  And soon fell asleep.

The ape got to five,
  And peeped everywhere.
He went to a cave,
  But the snake was not there.

A rope that he saw
   Seemed just like the snake.
But close up he found
   He'd made a mistake.

"An apple!" he said.
   "My, my," smiled the ape,
"An apple is better
   Than just a wee grape."

While taking a bite
   Of the apple's red skin,
He spotted the snake
   And shouted, "I win!"

His shout woke the snake,
   Who slid to the ground.
"What's that?" asked the snake.
   "Who's making that sound?"

When he saw what it was,
   He said, "You win the grape!
I'm glad to be safe.
   I had a close scrape."

Said the ape, "Hide-and-seek
   Is the game, Mr. Snake.
If you play hide-and-SLEEP
   You may not awake."

The Whale Who Liked Lemonade

A whale had a job at a zoo. He gave children rides on his back. He enjoyed his job, but he did not smile. One thing made him unhappy. "I like lemonade," he said to his pal the ape. "I have a real taste for it. But there's no lemonade at this zoo."

"I like lemonade too," said the ape, "but I like pineapples better. Let's go on a trip and get some pineapples and lemonade!"

So after bedtime, when the zoo keeper was asleep and children were home in bed, the ape hopped on the whale's back. They went to hunt for lemonade – and maybe some pineapples, too. The whale swam down the river until he came to the sea. There he saw a crab sitting on the beach.

"What's the matter, whale?" asked the crab. "You don't seem very happy."

"I'm not," said the whale. "I have a taste for lemonade. But I don't have any. Can you tell me where I can get some? And maybe some pineapples for the ape here?"

"Swim that way," said the crab, pointing south with a claw. "Go five miles past the green mountain. Soon you'll get your lemonade—and maybe some pineapples, too."

The whale swam five miles past the green mountain and soon had reached Africa. The ape jumped off the whale's back and ran into the trees seeking some lemonade and pineapples. He found a snake beside a cave.

"There's one thing making my pal unhappy," the ape said to the snake. "He wants some lemonade, but he doesn't have any. Can he get some here?"

"There's no lemonade here," said the snake.

"Any pineapples?" asked the ape.

"No," said the snake. "But go back to the sea. Swim south until the next sunrise. Go nine miles past the white mountain. Soon you'll get your lemonade—and maybe some pineapples, too."

The whale swam nine miles past the white mountain and soon had reached the South Pole. The ape on his back was shivering. The whale saw a man. He had a fishline in one hand.

"Something's making me unhappy," the whale said to the man. "I have this taste for lemonade. But I can't get any. Can I get some here?"

The man smiled. "Not here," he said. "Swim nineteen miles past the brown mountain. Soon you'll get your lemonade."

The whale swam and swam. The waves were like mountains, and the ape began to get seasick. Nineteen miles past the brown mountain, the whale saw flames. A boat was on fire.

"Help!" shouted a sailor. "Save us from the fire!"

The whale swam to the side of the boat and the sailors leaped down onto his back. Then, with his big tail splashing in the sea, he put out the flames.

"How can I thank you for putting out the blaze?" asked the captain.

"One thing would make me happy," said the whale. "I have a real taste for lemonade. But I don't have any. Where can I get some?"

"Why, that's easy," said the captain. "Swim to the pink mountain. Stop. You'll see the mouth of the White River. Swim up it and you'll get to a lake filled with lemonade."

The whale and the ape thanked the captain and waved to the sailors. Soon they arrived at the pink mountain. They found the mouth of the White River and swam up it.

There was a lake shaped like a valentine. It was nine miles wide and filled with lemonade. But something was floating in it. Big chunks of pineapple were floating in it! It was pineapple-lemonade punch!

The whale drank and drank and drank. The ape ate and ate and ate.

But then the whale said, "There's just one thing making me unhappy."

"What now?" asked the ape.

"I have no children to ride on my back."

So the whale swam back to the zoo, with the ape on his back. The children shouted with joy when they saw the whale coming home.

And now the whale has a wide smile. Children ride on his back each day. And whenever he wants lemonade, he knows where to get it—and some pineapples, too.

Cake and Lemonade

When I'm at home
Alone today,
I'll invite some pals
To come and play.

We'll ride our bikes
To the lake and back,
Then come inside
And have a snack.

I know they'll like
The cake I've made.
And wait till they taste
My lemonade!

__a__	
lazy	able
crazy	table
■	stable
baby	■
■	cradle
lady	■
■	aviator
bacon	alligator
■	radiator
apron	

__e__	
Steven	zebra
even	■
■	secret
evening	■
■	tepee
evil	■
■	Peter
Sweden	

__i__	
find	lion
kind	■
mind	dandelion
blind	■
grind	tidy
behind	■
■	tiger
mild	■
wild	spider
child	■
	pilot

__u__	
music	truth
■	■
pupil	ruin
■	■
tulip	July

__o__	
cold	hero
fold	zero
gold	■
sold	potato
told	tomato
scold	■
old	Eskimo
■	■
roll	radio
toll	■
troll	auto
■	■
most	hello
post	■
■	ago
poster	
■	
pony	
■	
open	
■	
only	

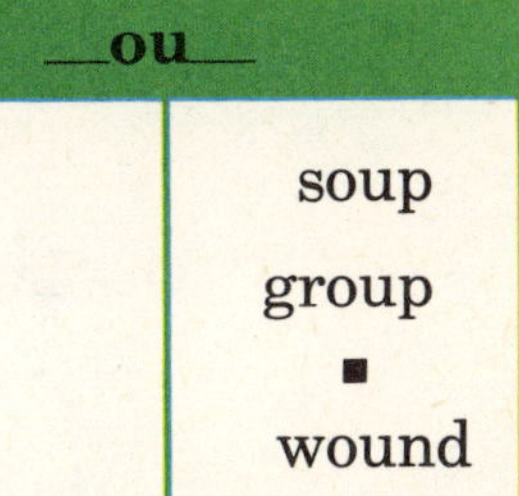

__ou__
soup
group
■
wound

__ow	
mow	fellow
row	yellow
bow	■
low	shadow
blow	■
crow	window
grow	
show	
slow	
snow	
throw	

Lion in the Snow

What would a lion do
  If by some mistake
In Africa it snowed
  While he was wide awake?

The lion would be quiet,
  Not knowing snow was real.
He'd reach an eager paw out
  To see how snowflakes feel.

What would a lion do
  If snow fell fast and wet?
He'd make himself a snowman,
  Then dine on him, I'll bet!

Manfred, the Unhappy Lion

Manfred was asleep in his home at the zoo one day. While he slept, Tammy the crow stopped by.

"Manfred, get up," Tammy scolded. "I've got something bad to tell you."

Manfred slowly lifted one golden paw. "I'm sleeping now. Come back later."

Tammy hopped over the windowsill and pecked at Manfred's rolled-up tail. "Manfred, the zoo keeper is going to throw you out of this zoo."

"Never," Manfred said, and he rolled over. "A zoo has to have a lion."

"They say they're going to get a baby lion," Tammy explained. "They'll put you behind the stable until you're sold to another zoo."

Manfred stopped in the middle of a yawn. He got up and ruffled his golden coat. Manfred was proud of the thick silky coat he had grown.

"What are you saying, Crow? Why do they want to sell me?"

Tammy pecked at the windowsill for a moment. Finally she said, "To tell the truth, Manfred, you're not as well liked by the children as some of the other animals. Not one child comes to your window."

"That's unkind," Manfred said sadly. He ruffled his coat. "I'm a very fine lion. Why, my coat is really golden, not yellow like others you see. It isn't easy to find a lion with a coat like mine."

Tammy liked Manfred. She didn't want to be unkind, but she had to speak. "Manfred, do you mind if I tell you something? Here's why I think you aren't well liked. You're lazy."

Manfred stopped yawning. "Lazy?" he said.

Tammy was trying to be polite. "Well, maybe not lazy, but you don't DO anything. Children like to see an animal do something besides show off his coat."

Manfred nodded sadly. "That may be, but what can I DO?"

"Well," said Tammy, "the baby tiger rolls over and over, and children run to his window just to see him. If children come to your window, I know the zoo keeper won't sell you."

"I can roll over as well as anyone," said Manfred. "But that's not my kind of fun. Still – if you really think it would help, I'll try it."

That day Manfred rolled over and over – many times.

But only one child came to see him. A grownup came too, but she said, "Come on, Pat, let's go. I'd rather see the alligator show his teeth."

By evening Manfred couldn't roll over. When Tammy came by, Manfred just lay there.

Tammy saw lots of leftover meat in Manfred's den. She could tell that Manfred didn't feel well.

"Hello, Manfred," said Tammy. "Are you sick?"

Manfred nodded. "I rolled over and over, but only one child came to my window. Now my sides are swollen and my coat is ruined. I'll be sold; I just know it."

"Be brave," said Tammy. "I'll try to think of something to help."

When the yellow sun began to glow on Manfred's windowsill, Tammy came back.

"Manfred," she said, "the alligator told me that children run to see him when he opens his mouth and shows his teeth. Show me your teeth."

Manfred opened his mouth. His two rows of teeth were white and pointed. "Like this?" he asked.

"Fine," said Tammy. "Show your teeth and you'll be as well liked as the alligator."

Manfred spent the day opening his mouth and showing his teeth. Many children did come to his window, but they didn't stay.

"He's too quiet," they told the grownups. "That can't be a real lion. Let's go see the tigers."

Later, Tammy hopped over to see Manfred. Manfred had his chin on his paws.

"Well?" Tammy said.

Manfred said, "They came to my window, but the children said I was too quiet."

"I know what," said Tammy. "How about singing?"

"I can't read music, and I don't know any tunes," said Manfred. He seemed about to cry.

"I'll help you," said Tammy, as kindly as she could.

Manfred got up slowly. "I don't think I can sing a note, but I'll try."

He opened his mouth. The only thing that came out was a low growl.

"Try another tune," said Tammy.

Manfred lifted his chin and opened his mouth. This time a loud growl rolled out.

"You see," he said, "I just can't sing."

"Wait," said Tammy. "See! There are rows and rows of children at your window. And behind them are rows and rows of grownups. Manfred, try to sing louder!"

Manfred got up. He ruffled his coat. He opened his mouth. Then he tried to sing louder. Out of his mouth rolled a terrible, loud GRR-OWL! The rows and rows of children smiled. The rows and rows of grownups smiled. Then they began to clap. It sounded like thunder.

"They like me! They like me!" Manfred said. He would have smiled but he didn't want to spoil his act.

"That's it!" said Tammy. "Manfred, now you'll never be sold!"

And it was the truth. Manfred was never sold—for he became the best-liked animal in the zoo. And when the baby lion came to the zoo, Manfred showed him how to growl.

And Tammy? Well, while the lions are growling, she has dinner. Manfred never forgets to save her some meat.

You're Invited

"Spiders are gay," said a spider.
  "We spin silky webs every day."
"How fine," said a fly most unkindly.
  "But I must stay out of your way."

"But spiders are kind," said the spider.
  "We're not lazy or silly or loud."
"Indeed," said the fly so politely.
  "Then you should be terribly proud."

"You'll be fine in my web," said the spider.
  "In MY web you'll never be cold."
"I know," the fly said in a whisper.
  "That web of yours has quite a hold."

"Then why not come over and visit?"
  Said the spider, "Have dinner, and see."
Said the fly, "I'd not mind just a visit.
  But I'm afraid dinner'd be me!"

Wendella the Witch

Wendella the Witch was lying on her king-size bed, playing music on her radio. Wendella was the only witch in her pack who had a king-size bed and a radio.

Wendella was the only witch who had a TV set and an electric toothbrush. She was the only witch who ate Chinese egg rolls and put on lipstick. Wendella liked being the only one. Wendella liked being different.

It was late October, and Halloween was just two days away. Wendella was asking herself what she could get that would make her different from the other witches this Halloween.

That's why she jumped up when the man on the radio said "electric broom."

"Electric broom?" said Wendella.

"Yes, I said electric broom." The man went on, "It's fast! It's easy! Just plug it in, flip the switch, and let it do the cleaning for you. See the latest model now – the Little Dragon electric broom!"

"Wow!" shouted Wendella. "An electric broom. Boy, I could really zoom around on that! And those other witches will have a fit!"

So Wendella went downtown that very day and got a Little Dragon electric broom.

On Halloween the witches met at Wendella's home. She was the proudest witch there. She showed her electric broom to her sister witches.

One of them, a witch named Twitch, said, "It's a grand broom, Wendella, but I don't think you should ride it. You see —"

But Wendella cut her off. "Just wait, Twitch," she said. "I'll be the slickest, swiftest witch in the sky. You'll see."

Then came the signal to take off. Wendella flipped the switch on her electric broom.

ZOOM! She went flying past the other witches and left them way behind.

TWANG! SNAP! CRASH! Wendella and her Little Dragon came back down with a bang.

Twitch zoomed back down to help.

"What happened?" asked Wendella.

"You got to the end of the electric power line, silly. You've only got twenty-five feet of line. I tried to tell you."

Wendella felt awful. The other witches were off casting terrible spells, and she was still on the ground.

"Get your old broom, Wendella, and let's go," said Twitch. "You used to do O.K. with your old broom."

"No," said Wendella. "I know what I'll do. My FM radio has a battery pack. I don't have to plug the radio in. I'll put the radio's battery pack on the electric broom. Then I won't have to plug the broom in. I won't need the power line."

"Wendella, why do you HAVE to be different?" asked Twitch. But it was no use.

Wendella put the battery pack on the broom and off she went. Now everything was fine. She sailed in the sky with a low humming sound. She zoomed up to the other witches and passed them by.

Then Wendella saw several boys down below. "O boy!" she cried. "Now for some fun!" She swooped down to cast one of her terrible spells. But just as she got close, there was a loud CLUNK. The electric broom jumped and rattled. The boys tried to see where the sound had come from. They saw Wendella and ran away.

"Rats and toads!" Wendella cried. She went on trying to find someone she could bewitch.

But the broom was getting louder every second. It was clunking and clanking and rattling. Each time Wendella got close to someone, the loud sounds would make him run away.

"Why won't this thing be quiet?" Wendella said. "I can't sneak up on anybody with this racket going on. Rats and toads!" She hadn't cast one spell yet.

Just then, Twitch went flashing by.

"Twitch! What's the matter with this thing?" Wendella shouted. "It's louder than a bagful of tin pans and mad cats! And it doesn't even want to go up over the treetops now. It's staying awfully low!"

Just then she smashed into the branch of a tree. She fell to the ground.

Twitch came down to help. "Are you O.K.?" she asked Wendella.

"I think so. But what's the matter with this rotten broom?"

Twitch checked it over. "For crying out loud, Wendella! Don't you know how an electric broom does its cleaning?"

"No," said Wendella. "How?"

"It sucks things up inside it, silly!" Twitch showed her. Inside the broom were two boys' hats, a crow, the crow's nest, an apron, some nuts and bolts, a pint of milk, a lady's wig, and a bowl of goldfish.

"With that junk inside, it couldn't help but crash," said Twitch.

"Well that does it!" said Wendella. "I'm dumping this junk-eater here. Can you let me have a ride home?"

"Hop on," said Twitch.

The next day Wendella and Twitch switched on the radio. A man was saying:

"There's no mistake about it. The witches were here by the hundreds. This town is upside down and inside out. What a mess!"

Sad Wendella! She hadn't cast one spell, and the other witches had had so much fun!

"What a wild, crazy thing that electric broom was," said Wendella. "I'm sticking to my old straw broom from now on." And she's done it too. Every Halloween, she gets on her old straw broom and casts the meanest spells in the land.

"The old ways are still the best ways," she likes to say.

But she still likes to be different. That's why she's made up her mind not to dress in black next Halloween. She's got a yellow evening gown, and she can't wait to put it on. So if you see a flash of yellow in the sky next Halloween, it's Wendella.

And if you see her—RUN!

If I Could Be

If I could be
  An Eskimo
And it was zero
  Or below,

I would not mind
  The wind and cold,
As Eskimos
  Do not, I'm told.

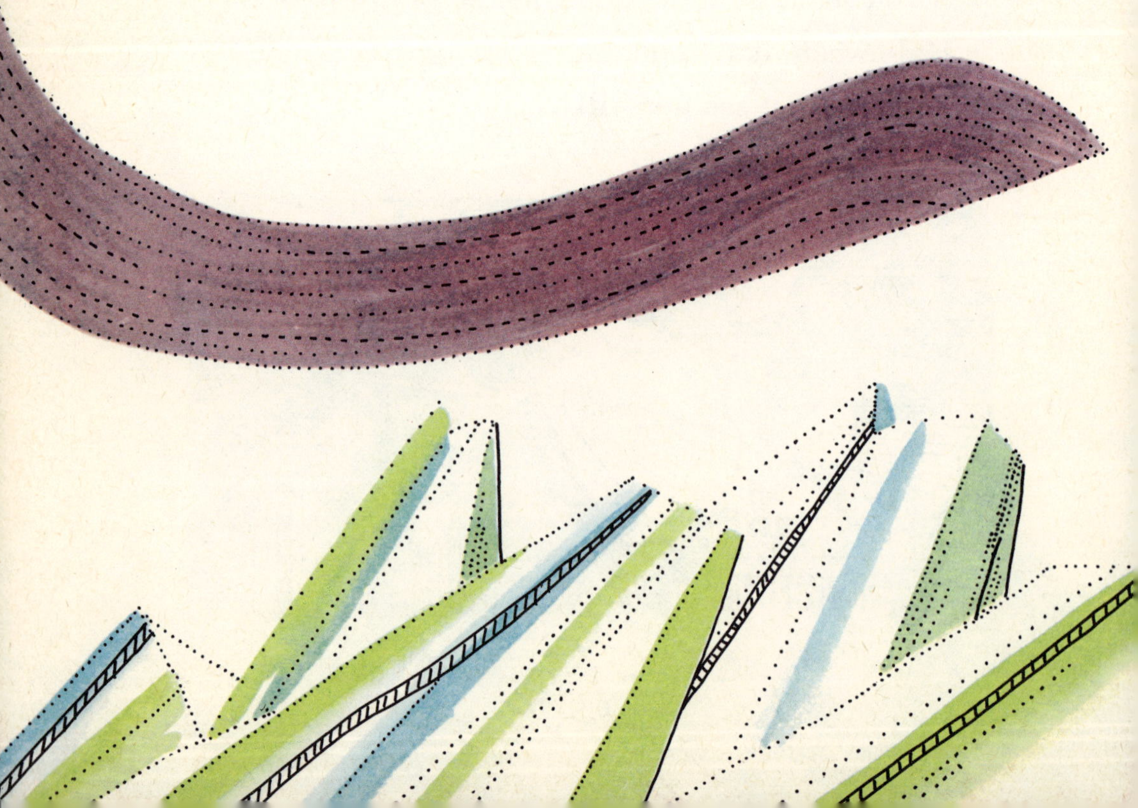

And if I were
  A goldenrod,
With gusts of wind
  I'd nod and nod.

And if I must
  A snowflake be,
A lazy snowman
  Make of me.

But I am just
  A little child.
I'm fine sometimes
  And sometimes wild.

Little Seal's Plane Ride

Little Seal, an Eskimo boy, was fishing a little way from his family's igloo. He was fishing in a hole in the frozen lake.

Little Seal didn't have much time to fish in the winter. In the Eskimo land of upper Canada, the sun shone only a little while each day.

It was snowing, and the wild wind was blowing. To Little Seal, however, this was a fine day for fishing. It was not as cold as most winter days.

Little Seal was waiting for the sound of the mail plane. It would be flying over soon. It came over every week with mail for the trading post, sixty miles from Little Seal's home. And this was the day.

"What would it be like in a plane?" Little Seal asked himself many times. He had never seen a plane on the ground—just up in the sky. He didn't know an Eskimo who had ever taken a ride in a plane.

Little Seal saw the plane at last. But it was flying low, much lower than it had on most other trips. Little Seal saw it drop even lower. It seemed that it was going to crash.

Little Seal jumped onto his dog sled. He shouted to his dogs. The dogs ran as fast as they could. Finally, they came to the spot where the plane had landed. The plane had flipped over in the snow and the pilot had rolled out. The plane was completely ruined.

"Am I glad to see you!" said the pilot. She was in pain. "My leg's broken. Can you help me?"

Little Seal helped the pilot onto the sled and put blankets of sealskin over her. The boy held the lead dog by the collar. He had to go slowly so the pilot would feel less pain.

When the sled got to the igloo, Little Seal's mother and father made a bed for the pilot. They put twigs on the snow. Then they put animal skins on top of the twigs.

The pilot said her name was Edith Brown. She had flown the mail many times, but had never crashed.

"When the sun comes up, the other pilots will try to find me," Miss Brown said. "We've got to find some way to let them know where I am."

The next day, at sunrise, Little Seal ran out in the snow and began stamping his feet. Soon he had stamped out EDITH'S HERE in the snow next to the igloo. He stayed there until the sun went down. But no plane came over.

Each day Little Seal stamped out EDITH'S HERE in the snow. And then one day a plane did come over. Little Seal waved and waved. He pointed to the igloo. At last the pilot saw him, and soon the plane landed on the snow on the lake. Little Seal ran up to the men in the plane and led them to the igloo.

Miss Brown thanked Little Seal and his mother and father. And she said to Little Seal, "I'll be seeing you, maybe sooner than you think."

Then she was taken to the plane on a stretcher. A moment later the plane was off the ground and flying away. Little Seal went back to his fishing.

One day, many weeks later, Little Seal saw the mail plane coming in as low as it had on the day of the crash. But this time it made a fine landing. It came to a stop next to where Little Seal was fishing. The pilot jumped out. It was Edith Brown.

"My leg has mended, and I'm back on the job today," the pilot said. "I couldn't forget the boy who was so kind to me when I needed help. Come on. Jump in, and we'll take a ride to the trading post and back."

Little Seal was the happiest boy in the land of the Eskimos as he sailed up into the sky.

I Like You, But—

"Will you be my valentine?"
  Said a lion to a cat.
"Not this evening," said the cat.
  "I'm afraid I have to scat."

"Will you be my valentine?"
  Lion asked a tiger then.
"Kind of you to ask, but no.
  I must go and dust my den."

Lion asked a zebra, too,
  "Will you be my valentine?"
"Rather not," the zebra said.
  "Have to clean my stripes at nine."

"Who will be my valentine?"
  Lion cried. "They just say no."
"Over here," a snake said then.
  "Over here! I think I know."

"I can't come," the lion said.
  So the old snake said, "You see?
Others are afraid of you
  Just as you're afraid of me."

How the Lion Got His Tail

Some time ago there was an ape with a tail of some size. And there was a lion with no tail of any size. No one knows when this was, for nobody can remember when an ape had a tail and a lion did not.

The ape's tail was fine for playing in the trees. He used his tail to hang from the branches. He used it to swing from tree to tree. He picked bananas with it. He stayed in the trees most of the time—and for a reason. The lion was forever trying to get the ape's tail.

One day the ape said to the lion: "Why are you so mean to me? Every day you try to steal my tail. Why do you want it?"

"If I had a fine tail," the lion said, "I could be the king of beasts and could sit on a throne."

"Never," said the ape. "The tiger is the king of beasts."

"He is now," said the lion. "But why should he be king forever? I'm bigger and better than the tiger. I'm even wiser than he is. There's just one thing he has that I don't have!"

"Stripes!" said the ape.

"Well, yes," said the lion. "But I have this big golden mane—and he doesn't have one. So I think we're even on that. There's just one other thing he has that I don't have."

"A tail," said the ape.

"Yes," said the lion. "That's it. The other animals agree that if I just had a big tail, I'd be the best animal around. And I would be king."

"I understand. And I'd like to help you," the ape said. "But I need my tail. Without it I wouldn't be able to play in the trees and swing on the vines. Why don't you try another tail? Why not the zebra's?"

"Now what would I do with a striped tail?" asked the lion. "Besides, the zebra's tail is too stubby."

The ape said, "The finest tail I know anything about is the peacock's. How about getting the peacock's tail?"

"I should say not!" the lion said. "It's fine behind a peacock. But can you see it behind me! Anyway, your tail is just the size and shape I need."

"I feel sorry for you, but I'm going to keep my tail," said the ape. And he swung up into the trees to eat some pineapples.

But soon after that, the ape fell asleep on a low branch. And wouldn't you know? He forgot to hang up his tail.

The lion came by and saw it hanging down. He was overjoyed. "This is the moment I've waited for!" he said. And he quickly snapped off the ape's tail and ran home with it.

The ape woke up and screamed, "Help! Help! The lion has my tail."

But the animal kingdom was silent and nobody came. Finally the ape sat down with no tail behind him.

"What shall I do now?" the ape asked himself. "I'd better find the other animals and tell them what happened. But how will I go? Maybe I can stand up on my two hind feet."

And he did. Slowly, slowly, he went from one animal to another to show them what had happened. He had never taken steps using only his two hind feet. He soon found out it was quite easy. And he could still go up trees easily by using his hands and feet. In fact, he began to think this way was better than the other.

"Let the lion have my tail," the ape shouted. "Let him be the king of beasts. Now that I can get about on two legs, I am like a man."

And that, it is said, is how the lion became the king of beasts—and why the ape has no tail.

Time to Grow

A caterpillar
Alone and slow
Becomes a butterfly,
You know.
It opens wide
Its wings and flies
To flowers, trees,
And rainbow skies.

The butterfly
Lays eggs and then
They hatch in time.
(They know just when.)
And who comes out
Of those eggs—who?
Why, baby caterpillars do!

The Wagon Master

This is the tale of Big Sam and Kit. It happened some time ago, when the American West was still open land. Not many homes were there yet. Travel to the West had just begun. Big Sam and Kit helped lead the way.

Kit was only seven. Her father, Big Sam, was a wagon master. It was Big Sam's job to lead the wagons. He had to pick the best trails to follow. He had to find the best streams for drinking.

The big wagons traveled slowly. They were loaded down with picks and axes and plows, kettles and pans. The travelers had to bring most of what they would need. When they got into the West, there would be no shops where they could get things.

After the wagons passed a wide river, they came onto the plains. There was blowing wind, and dust, and cold rain. There were snakes and stinging insects. The wagons were the only shelter. Tiny campfires were the only heat.

But the plains had fine soil for planting crops, and fresh, running streams. Some of the families wanted to stay.

"I think it's time we stopped," someone said. "This is rich land, and we could grow fine crops on it. We won't find a better home."

"And we need to rest," said another. "There's no reason to go on and on. I say we should stop here."

"Anyone who wants to stop here can stop," said Big Sam. "But I think I'll go on. There may be a better spot just beyond these plains."

Twenty families ended the trip there. The rest followed Big Sam and Kit over the plains.

There were Indians on the plains too. And they didn't want the settlers to come. The Indians were afraid they would ruin the land for hunting and fishing. The settlers were afraid of the Indians too. But even so, some of them wanted to stay.

"We don't know what the Indians will do," said one man. "But I still say we should stay here." Many of the others agreed with him.

Big Sam gazed at the mountains. "This is fine land," he said. "And there's plenty of food here. But there may be something better just behind those mountains. I think I'll go on."

The next day, twenty of the families stopped. The rest followed Big Sam and Kit into the mountains.

Winter was coming, and the trees were yellow and red in the mountains. As the wagons went up and up, it got colder. Soon there was snow. But there were spots between mountains where the travelers found shelter from the cold and snow.

"When spring comes," said one of the men, "we could put in crops here. Let's make a home in this spot." The others agreed. They were tired of traveling.

But Big Sam was studying the sky to the west. "What do you think?" he asked Kit.

"Well," said Kit, "there could be a better spot somewhere. And I'd like to see what's behind the mountains."

So Big Sam and Kit set out alone in the last wagon. And nobody knows what happened to them after that.

Every now and then, even today, someone claims to have seen a man like Big Sam with a child of about seven, traveling in a big wagon.

Sometimes they're seen on the plains, and sometimes in the mountains or on the desert. They seem to have traveled a lot. And they're still traveling.

Maybe it's Big Sam and Kit. Perhaps they are still trying to find a better spot.

How Many Golden Things There Are

What is golden, do you think?
  Goldenrod and a bobolink.
A goldfish is a yellow fellow,
  And dandelion, too, is yellow.

A maple leaf will put on gold
  In late October when it's cold.
And you can find some yellow in
  A lion's paw or tiger's skin.

From cats to stripes on a buzzing bee
  How many golden things we see!